Experience HIS Presence

A 63 Day Devotional & Journal

Life-Question Engagement Tool
Does God make my day?

prepared by
David A. Staff, Lead Pastor
Christ Community Church of Ames, IA

Table of Contents   Page

Life Questions

The Lord has given our Christ Community Church team 6 Life Questions to ask and answer regularly. They measure our participation in the team effort. They are:

- *Is the Spirit flowing through me?*
- *Does God make my day?*
- *Who shares my tough stuff?*
- *How worn is my welcome mat?*
- *With whom am I fishing?*
- *How are my investments doing?*

When spiritual teammates regularly **ASK** each other these questions, and seek to **GROW** in the personal application of these questions, together we "pull in the same direction." Prayerfully abiding in the Lord Jesus, we can be *very* fruitful in our ministry's mission.

Studies have discovered that developing a new habit takes between 60-70 days. Consistency over two months can imbed an important, even life-changing rhythm.

Core Principle: God is for me. Therefore a personal connection with the heart of God through prayer and the Scriptures gives me both passion and direction for life.

Helpful Evaluative Questions:

- *Do I regularly consult with God before entering my day/week/month/year?*
- *How often do I confer with God to the extent that it interrupts my plans?*
- *Do I regularly seek guidance from God through the Scriptures?*
- *Am I usually in a listening posture with God?*
- *How consistently do I humbly obey the voice of God?*

How To Use This Devotional Journal

The focus of this tool is the **2ⁿᵈ Life Question: *Does God make my day?***

Each page presents **a Biblical passage** focusing living each day in the presence of God, followed by **a short devotional reflection**. The **applicational question** (or questions) will help to focus a personal response. On an opposite page, there is ample room to **jot your thoughts** about growing in daily appointments with God, as well as to **write out your praying** to the Lord.

Each day, *spend 15-20 minutes before the Lord* to prayerfully and intentionally experience the near presence of the Lord himself. Take time to meditate on the reading and the thoughts which the Holy Spirit brings to mind. Write, reflect, apply, pray. When you complete the day's devotional, journaling your "conversation" with your heavenly Father, you can keep track using the upper right hand corner of the page, placing a ✓ in the box.

Each week, embedded in the journal every 7 days, you will find a page for you to summarize and review what the Spirit impressed on you in your week of times with the Lord.

Memorizing Key Scriptures

In addition to a consistent 63 day use of this devotional/journal, we can further renew our minds with several key Scriptures that emphasize the role of God's presence in our lives. So, set these to memory.

Proverbs 3:5-6

Trust in the Lord with all your heart, and do not lean on your own understanding. In all your ways acknowledge Him, and He will make straight your paths.

Mark 1:35

Then Jesus got up early in the morning when it was still very dark, departed, and went to a deserted place, and there he spent time in prayer.

John 15:7-8

If you abide in Me and My words abide in you, ask whatever you wish, and it will be done for you. By this is my Father glorified, that you bear much fruit, and so prove to be my disciples

1 John 1:5-7

This is the message we have heard from him and proclaim to you, that God is light, and in him is no darkness at all. If we say we have fellowship with him while we walk in darkness, we lie and do not practice the truth. But if we walk in the light, as he is in the light, we have fellowship with one another, and the blood of Jesus his Son cleanses us from all sin.

Acknowledgements

All Scripture quotations are taken from the Holy Bible, English Standard Version (ESV) copyright © 2001 by Crossway Bibles, a division of Good news Publishers. Used by permission.

Heartfelt thanks to Pamela Staff and Mark Chidister for their careful, helpful editing and format recommendations, to Jonathan Anderson for graphics and journal layout, and to Wayne Stewart for overall management of production. These are remarkable servants of the Master. My deep thanks as well for the many in the Christ Community Church family who prayerfully encouraged this project. Finally, praise be to the God who loves us, imparts His life to us by grace through faith, and thoroughly delights in our company as we delight in His.

David A. Staff, Lead Pastor
Christ Community Church of Ames, Iowa

Genesis 1:3-5, 2:2

And God said, "Let there be light," and there was light. And God saw that the light was good. And God separated the light from the darkness. God called the light Day, and the darkness he called Night. And there was evening and there was morning, **the first day**... And on the seventh day God finished his work that he had done, and he rested on the seventh day from all his work that he had done.

*(for fuller context, read **Genesis 1:1-2:3**)*

Perhaps we've never given it a second thought. Why day-by-day creating? (however you understand the word "day") Why not all at once? Why a rotating planet toggling back-n-forth between darkness and light? Evening, morning. Why the rhythm of one's energy spent, then needing our energy replenished through rest, followed by the renewed hope of fresh strength arriving with the dawns of each morning. With each 24 hour spin, a new day of possibilities?

Our marvelous Creator has crafted the cadence of our dependence. Like batteries requiring recharge, we exhale only to immediately need an inhale. Moment-by-moment, via the daily pulse, our Provider reminds us that what we truly need is what He alone can give. What He willingly gives we need day-by-day. Enough light on the path ahead, enough breath and strength for the day's work, enough manna for the day's meals, enough rest for the morrow's challenges (cf. Ps.127:2).

The Baptizer declared,

"A person cannot receive even one thing unless it is given him from heaven" (John 3:27).

Paul reminded Athen's incessant debaters,

"God himself gives to all mankind life and breath and everything"
(Acts 17:26).

Psalm 59:16 declares, "But I will sing of Your strength; I will sing aloud of Your stead-fast love in the morning." Meet with God each day. Sing loud His love. Recharge!

Questions:
*Am I willing to develop a daily habit of meeting with God?
Really?*

Thoughts:

Prayer:
For establishing a meeting rhythm with God...

Psalm 90:14
Satisfy us in the morning with your steadfast love,
that we may rejoice and be glad all our days.

Genesis 1:26-27

Then God said, "Let us make man in our image, after our likeness. And let them have dominion over the fish of the sea and over the birds of the heavens and over the livestock and over all the earth and over every creeping thing that creeps on the earth." So God created man in his own image, in the image of God he created him; male and female he created them.

*(for fuller context, read **Genesis 1:26-2:25**)*

Did you notice it? The word "our" comes out of nowhere. With whom is God talking? Shouldn't it read, "I'll make man in *my* image." And, when you think about it, God must be talking to…well, God. God alone has a "likeness" that is like nothing else, a likeness that has not been imprinted on any other portion of what He's just created (cf. Gen. 1:1-25).

Still, is God talking to Himself? He addresses another Person, or Persons. "Let's make man in OUR image." Our understanding of this conversation requires the larger revelation of Scripture. In the Bible's sacred pages, God reveals himself to be a Triune Being. There is One God who exists in 3 Persons: God the Father, God the Son, and God the Holy Spirit (cf. Is. 61:1, Matt. 28:19-20, 1 Cor. 12:4-7).

Fred Sanders helpfully writes:

> God is God in this way: God's way of being God is to be Father, Son, and Holy Spirit simultaneously from all eternity, perfectly complete in a triune fellowship of love. (*The Deep Things of God: How the Trinity Changes Everything*).

Created in His image, we human beings think, feel, and choose to pursue loving relationships because God Himself is a Being of Three Persons who think, feel, choose to love and relate with one another… and the desire to do so He has also imprinted in us.

So there is a God who has created you and wants a love-relationship with you!

Question:

Since love grows through sharing and relating, how might God and I grow our love relationship?

Thoughts:

Prayer:

For relating and sharing love with God...

Psalm 36:7
How precious is your steadfast love, O God!
The children of mankind take refuge in the shadow of your wings.

Genesis 2:7, 15-18

Then the LORD God formed the man of dust from the ground and breathed into his nostrils the breath of life, and the man became a living creature...The LORD God took the man and put him in the garden of Eden to work it and keep it. And the LORD God commanded the man, saying, "You may surely eat of every tree of the garden, but of the tree of the knowledge of good and evil you shall not eat, for in the day that you eat of it you shall surely die." Then the LORD God said, "It is not good that the man should be alone; I will make him a helper fit for him."

Though some today seek to devalue this account, the Spirit presents these remarkable moments as actual, factual history. Reflect on the wonder. The Uncreated One, the Lord God Himself, steps on to the planet He has shaped and continues to fashion. Suddenly, Divine Hands are plunged into soil while supernatural (yes, unfathomable!) craftsmanship, guided by limitless wisdom (cf. Prov.8:22), produces the greatest expression of His ﬡﬤﬠ (Heb., "creating"). Moments later, a mature human being, male in gender, lies in the grass.

The 2nd Person of the Trinity is not done. Purposefully, He bends low, almost as if to kiss, and personally "breathes" life into Adam's nostrils, filling his lungs, enlivening his soul, energizing his heart. Oh to have watched these moments! What was prone now sits, then stands, perhaps stretches (?), flowing with the fullness of endowed life. Opened eyes behold the LORD God, the Almighty, Maker of the heavens and the earth...an arm's length away.

"My Creator...not distant...present." Were these Adam's first thoughts? We are not told. Still, we see *God ushering* Adam to his home, explaining his calling, offering vast provision and defining the moral boundary. And then (significantly), *observing* that Adam needs unique help to obediently get after it.

Do we not yet today–each day–require a similar ushering from the Lord through the pathways of our daily lives?

Question:

Will I invite God to usher me, each day, through my challenges?

Thoughts:

Prayer:

For inviting God to guide me through each day's schedule...

Psalm 119:59
When I think on my ways, I turn my feet to Your testimonies

God's Provision and Guidance - 2

Genesis 2:8-9, 16-17

And the LORD God planted a garden in Eden, in the east, and there he put the man whom he had formed. And out of the ground the LORD God made to spring up every tree that is pleasant to the sight and good for food. The tree of life was in the midst of the garden, and the tree of the knowledge of good and evil…And the LORD God commanded the man, saying, "You may surely eat of every tree of the garden, but of the tree of the knowledge of good and evil you shall not eat, for in the day that you eat of it you shall surely die."

Beauty and bounty. Earth yet today exhibits the nascent provision which spread before the eyes of Adam. Then, an un-marred creation shone with the fantastic first-fruits of God's creative brilliance. It must have taken Adam's endowed breath away. "This is for you," Yahweh assured. "Partake obediently and avoid wisely."

Adam was bidden to experience all the potential, unlimited joys he could unlock and release from the material creation. Even the Tree of Life was his (it will be ours again in the eternal age, cf. Rev.22:2); he never need see anything end dismally in decay or death. A world, a universe, was before him to explore, to develop in holiness, to energize with excellent leadership. But there was a daily requirement. Simply, it was to faithfully rehearse the revelation from God. Then, obey the instruction of God. Result…a flourishing in the life of God.

Challenge lay ahead. Adam's sanctification would be tested by the subtlety of a wrongly-empowered serpent. Could the thankfulness welling up within the First Adam withstand the confusing, yet intriguing, offer to live independently, though disobediently? Would he succumb to idolizing the beauty, taste, and experience of the creation rather than reserving such worship for the Creator alone? Sadly, we know the answer. Nonetheless, daily joy is offered today through the same formula. Rehearse His revelation; simply obey… and flourish in true Life.

Question:

What of God's revelation should I be rehearsing and simply obeying? He planted trees and a granden so there was to eat for everyone to eat

Thoughts: He put me here and He Has planes for me by bring me to the hoase that Im in. He want's me to siver Him every day and keep me from bad things

Prayer:

For inviting God to guide me through each day's schedule...

Today Was a new clay and Help me to do right with all this.

---

1 Samuel 15:22

And Samuel said, "Has the LORD as great delight in burnt offerings and sacrifices, as in obeying the voice of the LORD? Behold, to obey is better than sacrifice."

Genesis 2:18-20

Then the LORD God said, "It is not good that the man should be alone; I will make him a helper fit for him." Now out of the ground the LORD God had formed every beast of the field and every bird of the heavens and brought them to the man to see what he would call them. Whatever the man called every living creature, that was its name. The man gave names to all livestock and to the birds of the heavens and to every beast of the field. But for Adam there was not found a helper fit for him.

John Sculley, an American executive for both PepsiCo and Apple, is credited with saying, "Timing in life is everything." Perhaps an exaggeration, timing nonetheless can be both critical and meaningful. Such is true in Genesis 2.

Note WHEN God states that Adam's aloneness is not good. It follows God's moral command to an alone–Adam to eat from all the trees except one. Eat from the one, and invite the intrusion of death into the vibrancy of life. Obeying God in these things was critical. One imagines Adam mulling God's words over in his heart. Yet it is THEN God says, "Adam's aloneness is not good. I will make him a helper corresponding for him." A helper for what?

We might instinctively think that Adam cannot reproduce by himself (which he couldn't). Or perhaps that he needed another worker–a hand with the development of Eden's beauty and fruitfulness (which, again, he did). But the timing of God's statement immediately follows the *moral command–the command requiring a moral choice each day to obey God by eating what was provided and not eating what was prohibited.*

While not every female is called into marriage, those who are do well to understand the call of God in being a husband's helper. She is given to help her husband live obediently and eagerly in the moral will of God. How important for them, daily, to help one another stay aligned with their Creator's revelation?

Questions:

If unmarried, what do I truly need in a mate? If married, what help do I critically need from my spouse? Are we meeting with God daily for this?

Thoughts:

Prayer:

For meeting with God with my spouse (present or future)...

Proverbs 12:4
An excellent wife is the crown of her husband

15

Genesis 3:1-3

Now the serpent was more crafty than any other beast of the field that the LORD God had made. He said to the woman, "Did God actually say, 'You shall not eat of any tree in the garden'?" And the woman said to the serpent, "We may eat of the fruit of the trees in the garden, but God said, 'You shall not eat of the fruit of the tree that is in the midst of the garden, neither shall you touch it, lest you die.'"

It is impossible to know how much Adam and Eve discussed what God had said to them before the incidents of this fatal chapter. The account suggests that

1. God directly gave <u>Adam</u> the command to be obeyed

2. God <u>never</u> directly spoke to Eve vocalizing the command

3. <u>Adam</u>, therefore, was <u>responsible</u> for communicating God's command accurately and clearly (presumably, they discussed *how* to obey and apply the command).

4. <u>Eve</u>, in her response to the Serpent, <u>added</u> <u>something</u> to the command given to Adam. [God never told Adam he could not *touch* the fruit of the Tree of Knowledge, rather that he could not eat it.]

Eve's addition is curious; its origin uncertain. Not surprisingly, the shrewd serpent saw in the "extra" (indicating a measure of confusion) an opening to further muddy the waters.

Have you ever felt our spiritual Enemy's attack in the form of uncertainty, confusion, lack of clarity over what God has actually said, prohibited, permitted? If so—and we all have—how much more important is it to spend time with God EACH day, giving His Spirit a chance to clarify and confirm the truth we have been given. We live by "every word that proceeds from the mouth of God" (Jesus, Matthew 4:4). And, we have the Spirit of Truth whose ministry is to teach us truth, remind us of truth, and to form Jesus in us through its life-changing application.

Questions:

How clear am I on the most important things God has revealed in His word? Could I explain...the gospel, simply? ...walking with God, clearly?

Thoughts:

Prayer:

For gaining clarity on what God has revealed...

John 17:17 (Jesus)
"Sanctify them in the truth; Your Word is truth."

Checking With God When Tempted

Genesis 3:4-6

But the serpent said to the woman, "You will not surely die. For God knows that when you eat of it your eyes will be opened, and you will be like God, knowing good and evil." So when the woman saw that the tree was good for food, and that it was a delight to the eyes, and that the tree was to be desired to make one wise, she took of its fruit and ate, and she also gave some to her husband who was with her, and he ate.

Numbed by the modern swirl of untruths whipping through our minds on any given day—the endless onslaught—it may be we are wholly desensitized to recognizing when someone calls God Himself a liar. "God has held out on you, Eve," the serpent presses. "He has not let you in on the entire story. Violating His prohibition has nothing to do with your demise. Disobedience will hardly end in death. It has everything to do with God wanting no rivals on *insider* knowledge and experience. He simply wants to 'keep you in your place.' C'mon girl… you're better than merely taking God's words at face value!"

Genesis' account of Satan's ruse darkens, dimmed by two silences. First, Adam's silence. The leader is speechless, quiet, retiring. Standing next to Eve (note: "who was with her") Adam fails to correct or protect. Personally given God's Word, he retires from applying God's Word. Second, Eve's silence. Why not ask Adam, "Should we do this?" Why not caution, "Let's ask God when He visits later today." All that echoes in the void is the serpent's offer to become like God by violating God's revelation.

Suddenly, Eve leans, fascinated with the forbidden tree's alleged assets: *good* food, *delightful* fruit, *instant* insight. Sin is slippery quick; momentum in disobedience draws another in. "She ate… he ate." Quietly, tragically, death quickly strides through the opened door.

Question:

When tempted, do I first turn to the clear Word of God and ask my Father for perspective?

Thoughts:

Prayer:

For handling the slippery temptation my Enemy offers...

Matthew 6:13
"Lead us not into temptation, but deliver us from evil."

"Does God Make My Day?"
Journal Summary Week 1

Day 1   We Need God Daily - Genesis 1:3-5, 2:2

Day 2   Created By A Relational God - Genesis 1:26-27

Day 3   God's Provision and Guidance 1 - Genesis 2:7, 15-18

Day 4   God's Provision and Guidance 2 - Genesis 2:8-9, 16-17

Day 5   *God's Provision and Guidance 3 - Genesis 2 :18-20*

Day 6   *Clarity About God's Revelation - Genesis 3:1-3*

Day 7   *Checking With God When Tempted - Genesis 3:4-6*

In what way has the Lord urged me to change, or obey, this week?

Joy In Meeting With God

Genesis 3:7-8

Then the eyes of both were opened, and they knew that they were naked. And they sewed fig leaves together and made themselves loincloths. And they heard the sound of the LORD God walking in the garden in the cool of the day, and the man and his wife hid themselves from the presence of the LORD God among the trees of the garden.

In Romans 2:15, Paul describes our conscience's turmoil. "The work of God's law is written on their hearts, while their conscience bears witness, and their conflicting thoughts accuse or even excuse them..." Disregarding and disobeying God is no prescription for inner peace. Rather, it further ratchets up our soul's chaos.

Chaotic guilt drives Adam and Eve from open freedom into closeted fear. Worse, God once again sounds his daily arrival. Crouching low, sin produces even greater foolishness. "Perhaps He won't find us," Adam whispers. As their grandchildren, we repeat the silliness when putting created things between us and a relentlessly searching Creator. Stuff never provides much of a hiding place.

Positively, Genesis implies that the LORD God came every day for warm, renewable, life-giving interaction is with those He created in His image. The earliest weeks signaled what followed centuries later: God would incarnate. He loves being with people.

Negatively, the first couple forfeited the natural flow of holy joy at the prospect of seeing God. "Woe is me," Isaiah lamented, "I am unclean" (Is.6). Generations would now all begin in hiding before being found (cf. Ps. 51:5, Rom.3:23).

Thankfully, Jesus has changed all that for the one who lives by faith in the Sacrificed Lamb. Clothed in His righteousness, we are invited to come boldly into the Presence (cf. Heb.4:14-16), every day, every hour, every moment.

Question:

Am I eager for my daily, life-renewing meeting with God?

Thoughts:

Prayer:

For eagerness to meet the Lord daily...

Psalm 54:4
Behold, God is my helper; the Lord is the upholder of my life.

Needing God Even More

Genesis 3:9-11

But the LORD God called to the man and said to him, "Where are you?" And he said, "I heard the sound of you in the garden, and I was afraid, because I was naked, and I hid myself." He said, "Who told you that you were naked? Have you eaten of the tree of which I commanded you not to eat?"

What a curious triad of verses! I wonder if Moses smiled as the Spirit prompted his ancient scribal tool? God not knowing where the man was? Ha! God unaware who had beguiled? Ridiculous! The design behind Divine questions is never to mine for unknown information. Rather, they goad us into required self-assessment, confession, an accountability unto maturity. God's passionate probing harbors no interest in playing hide-n-seek games. "You desire truth in the inward being," David realizes (Ps.51:6). "You teach me wisdom in the secret heart."

If we sinfully disobey, God comes looking for us every day. He loves us too much to leave us–unbidden, guilt-ridden, alone–at the mercy of sin's degenerating destruction. Yes, He does give men over to the consequences of chosen evil (cf. Rom.1:24-32), but not without patiently, kindly, daily offering all humans clear, revealed truth coupled with the option of repentant gratefulness (cf. Rom.1:19-21).

Well-watered Eden would too quickly lose its first blessed residents (Gen.1:23). Sin's consequences (Gen.3:14-19) negatively complicate everything: nature uncooperative (if not dangerous), work difficult, relationships strained, child-birth agonizing, family-life combative, discordant. God's tree of life inaccessible. Ignoring God a perpetual legacy, daily living a *spiritual* battle.

More than ever, Adam and Eve, and their children, needed God's presence and provision. Eve realized her first child came "with the help of the Lord." In a more-difficult-than-intended world, it is ours to seek His help every day, in every way.

Question:

What are the difficulties I face requiring more of God every day?

Thoughts:

Prayer:

For God's presence in my daily challenges...

Psalm 6:4
Turn, O Lord, deliver my life.
Save me for the sake of your steadfast love.

Genesis 4:4-7

And the LORD had regard for Abel and his offering, but for Cain and his offering he had no regard. So Cain was very angry, and his face fell. The LORD said to Cain, "Why are you angry, and why has your face fallen? If you do well, will you not be accepted? And if you do not do well, sin is crouching at the door. Its desire is for (or, against) you, but you must rule over it."

Once again, we rightly find amazement in a God who personally reaches out to someone wrapped up in the small world of personal sin nurtured by self-justifying anger. Attempting to lift Cain from imprisoning frustration to freeing self-awareness, the Lord again uses questions as He did with Cain's father (cf. see previous devotional). Kidner comments:

In the Lord's repeated 'Why...?' and 'If...', His appeal to reason and His concern for the sinner are as strongly marked as His concern for truth (4:5a) and justice (4:10) [Genesis, p.75].

Through God's inquiring concern, Cain has opportunity for a life-giving, mid-course correction of heart and action. His Creator's assessment of what crouches nearby, ready to attack and dominate, needs to be taken seriously. God speaks to us in our failure to correct, restore, and protect, though we may mistakenly interpret His intrusion as Divine piling on. The filter-problem is ours. Yet choosing humility when hearing the Lord's voice can be the first step which rescues. So warned, and rightly postured with a lowly, teachable spirit, we may dominate sin's danger.

The Hebrews' author urged, "Today, if you hear His voice, do not harden your hearts, as in the rebellion" (i.e.,3:7, Israel's experience in the desert). No temptation–internal or external–lacks an escape hatch (cf. 1 Cor. 10:13). God is always nearby, asking good questions, pointing the way toward righteousness.

Questions:

When God's Spirit convicts me of sin, how do I respond?
Do I listen?

Thoughts:

Prayer:

For a humble heart when hearing the Lord's voice...

James 1:22,25
But be doers of the word, and not hearers only, deceiving
yourselves...a doer who acts will be blessed in his doing.

Genesis 4:8-11

Cain spoke to Abel his brother. And when they were in the field, Cain rose up against his brother and killed him. Then the LORD said to Cain, "Where is Abel your brother?" Cain said, "I do not know; am I my brother's keeper?" And the LORD said to Cain, "What have you done? The voice of your brother's blood is crying to me from the ground. And now you are cursed from the ground, which has opened its mouth to receive your brother's blood from your hand."

I've done it. You've done it. Cain did it. You hear from the Lord, only to-quite strangely-do *nothing* about what was just heard. At best we postpone doing what the Lord directed; at worst we dismiss it as inapplicable "in my case." God grants the freedom to choose a "yes" or "no" to His directive. Oddly, we often feel empowered to ignore. In doing so, we take a step further into sin. Such is the liability of being a son of the First Adam.

Moses doesn't disclose what Cain said to Abel immediately following the elder's flashing-yellow-light encounter with God. The LXX (ancient Greek translation of *Genesis*) has Cain making an appointment, adding: "Let us go out to the field." If historical, his words suggest a deliberate, plotted, disobedient response to God's warning. Cain follows the leadership of his flesh, a private plan gestated in anger and born in violent rage. Not satisfied merely to end a brother's life, Cain sheds blood (one can see a forecast of how Israel's angry elders would destroy their own kin-their Messianic son-centuries later).

In grace, the Lord *again* meets and speaks with Cain. More questions. Another opportunity for repentance. Sadly, again, Cain mimics his father evasiveness (cf. Genesis 3:12), yet minus the qualified admission. His impenitence is met with brutal disclosure and consequences. Nothing good results from sinning. By Divine action, the very ground Cain relies on for a living becomes all-the-more his adversary. However, though judged, mercy protects (Gen.4:15). Kidner:

"It is the utmost mercy can do for the unrepentant"
(*Genesis*, p.76).

Questions:

*When have I experienced God's mercy even though unrepentant?
What should I be learning from Cain's meeting with God here?*

Thoughts:

Prayer:

For a humble heart when hearing the Lord's voice...

Romans 2:4
Do you presume on the riches of his kindness and
forbearance and patience, not knowing God's kindness
is meant to lead you to repentance?

Genesis 5:21-24

When Enoch had lived 65 years, he fathered Methuselah. Enoch walked with God after he fathered Methuselah 300 years, and had other sons and daughters. Thus all the days of Enoch were 365 years. Enoch walked with God, and he was not (found), for God took him.

A human being's average lifespan in the early centuries of humanity, according to the Hebrew Scriptures (cf. Genesis 5), was 907½ years; twelve times longer than the present lifespan. Moses' records are purposefully crafted. Men had their first sons at a certain age (noted) only to, after that age, father more sons and daughter. Moses' account almost always records this minimal data. Except in one case.

Enoch too had his first son, Methuselah (who would become the world's oldest living man) at age 65. But suddenly, an extra description is added. After his first son was born, Enoch *walked with God*. Arguably, the only man among tens of thousands (or more) identified as so doing. Marcus Dods observes:

> *"Enoch walked with God because he was God's friend and liked God's company…because he was going in the same direction as God, and had no desire for anything but what lay in God's path."*

Why Enoch started to walk with God is unstated. Perhaps it was fathering his first child. This should get every man's attention, though for so many, a sin-dimmed outlook can devalue even this incredible opportunity. Perhaps when God spoke to him about His holiness and coming judgment (cf. Jude vss. 14-15), Enoch's heart uniquely quartered good soil. The word implanted produced fruit.

It seems that each and every day Enoch walked with God. So closely that his own lifespan fell short by 542.7 years. Why? So close to God, one day God just said, "No need to die. Just come on home…"

Questions:

Am I going where God is going? When I'm gone, will others say of me, "_____ just walked home with God?"

Thoughts:

Prayer:

For a deepening, daily walk with God...

Deuteronomy 5:33a
You shall walk in all the way that the Lord your God
has commanded you, that you may live...

Genesis 12:7-8

Then the LORD appeared to Abram and said, "To your offspring I will give this land." So he built there an altar to the LORD, who had appeared to him. From there he moved to the hill country on the east of Bethel and pitched his tent, with Bethel on the west and Ai on the east. And there he built an altar to the Lord and called upon the name of the LORD.

If you take the time to read from Genesis 12:1, you understand the pioneering spirit within the father of our faith (cf. Rom.4:11-12). An eager reader longs for additional detail. How did God first appear to Abram? How could Abram – for years (presumably) worshiping pagan deities – be certain the true God filled his heart's ears with directives? Since Abram left his home and culture *not knowing where he was going* (cf. Heb.12:8), in what way(s) did God provide the day-by-day vector?

Impressive is what Abram did when God finally put up the "Welcome Home!" banner. Abram built altars each place God appeared to him and spoke. The first the Oak of Moreh (12:6-7; must have been an impressive tree!). A new place of worship in the midst of thousands of godless Canaanites. The second between Bethel and Ai, near his tent (12:8).

Even more impressive is the final phrase in vs. 8: "...and *called upon the name of the Lord.*" Years ago, my Hebrew language teacher offered an insight. "This **called upon** can also be translated **declared.**" Significance? Abram's worship was not merely for his own personal enrichment. Likely Abram was introducing his Canaanite neighbors to the LORD–to *Yahweh*–the personal, unique name of God emphasizing both His promise-keeping and His desire for relationship. The LORD had kept his promise to Abram; He and Abram were in relationship.

Questions:
Do I see worship-time with God as for more than just my own personal enrichment? How can I share my relationship with God with others who need Him?

Thoughts:

Prayer:
For sharing my relationship with God...

Isaiah 41:8,10
But you, Israel my servant, Jacob whom I have chosen,
the offspring of Abraham, my friend...fear not, for I am with you.

Friendship With God - 1

Genesis 18:17-19, 22-25

The LORD said, "Shall I hide from Abraham what I am about to do, seeing that Abraham shall surely become a great and mighty nation, and all the nations of the earth shall be blessed in him? For I have chosen him, that he may command his children and his household after him to keep the way of the LORD by doing righteousness and justice, so that the Lord may bring to Abraham what he has promised him."...Abraham still stood before the LORD.

Then Abraham drew near and said, "Will you indeed sweep away the righteous with the wicked? Suppose there are fifty righteous within the city. Will you then sweep away the place and not spare it for the fifty righteous who are in it? Far be it from you to do such a thing, to put the righteous to death with the wicked, so that the righteous fare as the wicked! Far be that from you! Shall not the Judge of all the earth do what is just?"

Why God feels the need to consult with anyone about anything He needs to do reveals mystery. Yet such a mystery unfolds here. Honoring His friendship with Abram, Yahweh takes minutes to air it out with His friend (cf. 2 Chronicles 20:7, James 2:23b). Did Abraham feel compassion for people despite their entrenched debauchery? Acknowledging God's righteousness, this patriarch respectfully leverages God's merciful heart to extend more and more grace. At the same time, God demonstrates that indeed the Judge of all the earth is supremely just.

In the end, only three make it out of the wickedness—Lot and two grown daughters (Gen. 14:24-26,30)—only to perpetuate the fornication in the cave of rescue (14:31-38). As the fiery consumption finished, the Lord and Abraham stand together on a rise in early morning hours. Smoke, fire flashes, charred buildings and bodies envelop the landscape. The God Abraham knew was both patient and powerful. Always true to His word. Always worthy of believing. Also...always ready to disclose and discuss His will with those who draw near.

Question:
*What do I need to discuss with God about today...
and the future?*

Thoughts:

Prayer:
For understanding God's intentions in my life...

John 15:15 (Jesus)
"No longer do I call you servants, for the servant does not know
what his master is doing; but I have called you friends."

"Does God Make My Day?"
Journal Summary Week 2

Day 8   *Joy In Meeting With God - Genesis 3:7-8*

Day 9   *Needing God Even More - Genesis 3:9-11*

Day 10   *Hearing From God 1 - Genesis 4:4-7*

Day 11   *Hearing From God - 2 - Genesis 4:8-11*

Day 12 *Walking Closely With God - Genesis 5:21-24*

Day 13 *Daily Worship & Proclamation - Genesis 12:7-8*

Day 14 *Friendship With God 1 - Genesis 18:17-19, 22-25*

In what way has the Lord urged me to change, or obey, this week?

Genesis 22:10-12

Then Abraham reached out his hand and took the knife to slaughter his son. But the angel of the LORD called to him from heaven and said, "Abraham, Abraham!" And he said, "Here I am." He said, "Do not lay your hand on the boy or do anything to him, for now I know that you fear God, seeing you have not withheld your son, your only son, from me."

During my 10-year run with Coach Dan McCarney as chaplain for the Iowa State University football team, I (David Staff) delivered many a 15-minute chapel talk. Coach desired something spiritual just before the team boarded the bus for the stadium. For reasons I cannot today recall, one such talk focused on Abraham's tenacious willingness to obey and honor God...no matter what. To obey even if it meant the sacrificial slaughter of his only natural-born son.

You're thinking, "You unpacked Abraham's stunning obedience in a 15 minute talk? Are you kidding me?" No doubt full justice to the ancient episode was not served, but one young coach felt the impact. Trina had just delivered their firstborn, a beautiful boy, the unquestionable delight of this young coach's heart. Later, in the locker room, Tony looked me in the eye to say, "I could never obey God if He asked that of me." "Yeah," I replied. "Abraham's faith was amazing."

God's request called for graduate-level trust, but it was not issued in a vacuum. God and Abraham had been friends for 40 years. Been through thick and thin. Victories, failures, fantastic promises from God met with a growing confidence in God. Hebrews 11 indicates that Abraham was willing to obey even this request because he unflinchingly trusted God to raise Isaac from the dead, out of the ashes of his sacrifice (cf. Heb.11:19). While Abraham's feelings are not recorded, his obedience is--the product of daily, weekly, monthly, yearly investments in a trusting friendship with God. And the Spirit does not shrink from calling us to developing—day after day—that same kind of faith-filled friendship.

Question:

How does my obedience to God display my friendship with Him?

Thoughts:

Prayer:

For growing in trusting obedience of what God asks...

Hebrews 11:13, 16
These all died in faith, not having received the things promised
(yet)...God is not ashamed to be called their God.

Acting Without Consulting God

Genesis 25:29-34

Once when Jacob was cooking stew, Esau came in from the field, and he was exhausted. And Esau said to Jacob, "Let me eat some of that red stew, for I am exhausted!" (Therefore his name was called Edom.) Jacob said, "Sell me your birthright now." Esau said, "I am about to die; of what use is a birthright to me?" Jacob said, "Swear to me now." So he swore to him and sold his birthright to Jacob. Then Jacob gave Esau bread and lentil stew, and he ate and drank and rose and went his way. Thus Esau despised his birthright.

Abraham's twin grandsons grew within, and then were birthed from, a daughter-in-law's womb, scrapping about who would be first.

Gen. 25:22 The children struggled within Rebekah, and she said, "If it is thus, why?"

Crimson Esau emerged first even as supplanting Jacob clawed at his heel. Prophecy assured, and practice proved, the relentless competition between brothers for supremacy.

The critical incident reported above is unsurprising in one sense. Jacob, better at seizing opportunity, craftily capitalized on his brother's vacillating passions. Flesh-driven, Esau quickly, unthinkingly, forfeits what is irreplaceable. "Food for the stomach, and the stomach for food!" similarly motivated Christians chant in Corinth (1 Cor. 6:13). The priceless rewards and commendation for living by faith readily pawned for a single meal (cf. Heb.12:16), and subsequent (irreversible) rejection.

Surprising is the lack of consultation with God by either of the boys. The unfolding story contains no hint of inquiry, no "*LORD* God, should I do this? Does this advance Your purposes in my life? In my brother's life? Our family? The world?" How second-nature for us to recognize an opportunity for personal gain (even at the dis-advantage of a family member) and quickly go for it. Years of relational wreckage twisted itself around these two brothers, the bitter fruit of forgetting to simply meet with God and ask Him for counsel.

Question:

In decisions I make which effect my relationships, am I spending time with God to glean His direction and advice?

Thoughts:

Prayer:

For God's counsel in my dealings with others...

Proverbs 18:19
A brother offended is more unyielding than a strong city,
and quarreling is like the bars of a castle.

Grappling With God

Genesis 32:24-32

And Jacob was left alone. And a man wrestled with him until the breaking of the day. When the man saw that he did not prevail against Jacob, he touched his hip socket, and Jacob's hip was put out of joint as he wrestled with him. Then he said, "Let me go, for the day has broken." But Jacob said, "I will not let you go unless you bless me." And he said to him, "What is your name?" And he said, "Jacob." Then he said, "Your name shall no longer be called Jacob, but Israel, for you have striven with God and with men, and have prevailed."

Perhaps 600 years-old, dating to a phrase from Chaucer, the proverb "Chickens always come home to roost" reminds that hens forage outside during the day, yet habitually return to their nests in the evening. Meaning? "Your offenses toward others most certainly rebound back to you."

An anxious Jacob may not have tended chickens, but the imminent rebound of his deceptive cheating of brother Esau neared. An ominous scouting report: "Esau is coming to meet you; He has 400 men with him." *Then Jacob was greatly afraid and distressed* (Gen. 32:6). His untethered imagination tried to estimate how much bitterness was still burning within his twin. Slim the chances for a positive reunion. Jacob's options for self-preservation vaporized in his fright.

That night, alone on Jabbok's far side, an unknown man not only appeared but attacked. Wrestling is desperate engagement. Ancient wrestling often ended in the complete incapacitation, if not death, of the opponent. They wrestled till sunrise. For hours. Born tenacious, Jacob exerted what physical leverage he could muster. Advantage Jacob! until...until the man successful dislocated his hip. Now, pain knifed through a limp limb, and in early morning light, the Opponent insisted the match conclude. But had it dawned on Jacob his nocturnal Foe was his God (or, at least, God's messenger. The pre-incarnate Son?). Clenching harder, a desperation for God's help cried out, "No! First *bless* me!" Grappling acutely with God–the exercise Jacob's uncertain soul needed for peace.

Day 17 ■
Check when complete

Question:

When troubled, am I willing to wrestle with God for His blessing?

Thoughts:

Prayer:

For wrestling with God when unsure, uncertain...

Psalm 144:15
Blessed are the people to whom such blessings fall!
Blessed are the people whose God is the LORD!

Meeting the Burning Bush God - 1

Exodus 3:1-5

Now Moses was keeping the flock of his father-in-law, Jethro, the priest of Midian, and he led his flock to the west side of the wilderness and came to Horeb, the mountain of God. And the angel of the LORD appeared to him in a flame of fire out of the midst of a bush. He looked, and behold, the bush was burning, yet it was not consumed. And Moses said, "I will turn aside to see this great sight, why the bush is not burned." When the LORD saw that he turned aside to see, God called to him out of the bush, "Moses, Moses!" And he said, "Here I am." Then he said, "Do not come near; take your sandals off your feet, for the place on which you are standing is holy ground."

Our God, we are told, is a consuming fire (Heb.12:29). He also can inhabit fire designed not to consume but to miraculously, and unmistakably, communicate (cf. Acts 2:3). When He does, we do well to turn aside, take off our dirty sandals, and listen. To a God with a message and to a God who knows our name, our circumstances, and our usefulness to His purposes.

Moses desired discovery. Why was the scrub bush not reduced to a charred stump? Have you ever wondered why God chose to gain Moses' interest in this way? The bush itself–least among the wilderness growths–had little value, yet enflamed with the presence and voice of God. "God called him *out of the* bush." Moses would not soon forget this remarkable encounter with a nearly worthless shrub, the unlikely instrument of a God whose holiness could consume if someone with sin ventured too close.

But there was a way to come closer, or at least to belong in the presence of God. "Take your sandals off your feet." Ancient eastern practice insisted on removing one's sandals as a confessional act, one which acknowledges the need for a sovereign's grace and blessing, and readiness to hear from the one who is greater. Each day, we too have the opportunity to draw near, on ground made holy by the presence of God. With hearts that need grace, with ears ready to hear what the Fire has to say about His purposes in our lives. Here we are…

44

Day 18 ■
Check when complete

Questions:
Are my "sandals off" in God's presence? Ready to listen?

Thoughts:

Prayer:
For God to get my attention on His holy ground...

Hebrews 4:16
Let us then with confidence draw near to the throne of grace.

Exodus 3:4-6

When the LORD saw that Moses turned aside to see, God called to him out of the bush, "Moses, Moses!" And he said, "Here I am." Then he said, "Do not come near; take your sandals off your feet, for the place on which you are standing is holy ground." And He said, "I am the God of your father, the God of Abraham, the God of Isaac, and the God of Jacob." And Moses hid his face, for he was afraid to look at God.

What does it mean? When God calls out our name, twice? Anything? Examples happen at critical times. Moments when God refuses dismissal. When something urgent requires realization, embracing, worship, action.

As Abraham raised the knife to obediently sacrifice Isaac (Gen. 22:11), God's angel called to him from heaven "Abraham, Abraham! Do not lay your hand upon the boy or do anything to him, for now I know that you fear God..."

When Israel (formerly named Jacob) sacrificed to God at Beersheba wondering about his future, God spoke in a vision, "Jacob, Jacob... do not be afraid to go down to Egypt. There I will make of you a great nation" (Gen. 46:1-4).

Unfamiliar with God's voice, Israel's future prophet/judge heard in the night's stillness, "Samuel! Samuel!" (1 Sam. 3:1-10). Preoccupied with serving, perturbed by a sister not sharing her stress, Jesus' friend would hear, "Martha, Martha," (Lk. 10:38-42) "you are worried about unnecessary things." To Peter, "Simon, Simon–Satan demands to sift you like wheat" (to expose your chaff!) (Luke 22:31-32.)

Headstrong, blinded in hatred, he heard, "Saul, Saul, why persecute Me?" (Acts 9).

Most, when hearing their name twice, replied, "Here I am." In your quiet time with God today, listen for your name. Present yourself to God. Bend the knee. Listen for more. He has something important for you in your future.

Questions:
May God want my attention today in a special way?
Does He have it?

Thoughts:

Prayer:
To listen for my name and God's calling...

1 Samuel 3:9
"If He calls you, you shall say, 'Speak, LORD. Your servant hears.'"

Meeting the Burning Bush God - 3

Exodus 3:6-8, 10-12

And he said, "I am the God of your father, the God of Abraham, the God of Isaac, and the God of Jacob." And Moses hid his face, for he was afraid to look at God. Then the LORD said, "I have surely seen the affliction of my people who are in Egypt and have heard their cry because of their taskmasters. I know their sufferings, and I have come down to deliver them out of the hand of the Egyptians and to bring them up out of that land to a good and broad land....

Come, I will send you to Pharaoh that you may bring my people, the children of Israel, out of Egypt." But Moses said to God, "Who am I that I should go to Pharaoh and bring the children of Israel out of Egypt?" He said, "But I will be with you, and this shall be the sign for you, that I have sent you: when you have brought the people out of Egypt, you shall serve God on this mountain."

Those who meet with God regularly soon realize that such encounters are usually for more than just hanging out. Isn't that what the disciples discovered during days with God's Son? Sure, there were times Jesus said, "Come aside and rest" (Mark 6:31). But, quite often, time with Jesus meant yet another opportunity to both recharge and gain clarity about the challenge ahead, offering enslaved-to-sin people forgiveness with an invitation into the kingdom.

Moses sensed God's fearful greatness even as the I AM uttered His identity. The words were also reassuring; this God had not forgotten his covenant with the Fathers. It was time to deliver from bondage and envision a future. God's plan required a commissioned spokesman–one going, speaking, delivering–accompanied by the presence of God. Six words made all the difference–"But I will be with you." To be sure, Moses struggled to say "yes," but God would not give him a pass. "I have come down to deliver," the Lord said, "I'm sending you."

"Who will go for us?" asks God lifted-up. "Here am I," Isaiah offers. "Send me."

Questions:

When meeting with God, how willing am I to be sent to someone who needs the Lord's deliverance? How eager my "Send me!"?

Thoughts:

Prayer:

For readiness in God's sending...

John 20:21 (Jesus)
"As the Father has sent me, even so I am sending you."

Exodus 33:7-9

Now Moses used to take the tent and pitch it outside the camp, far off from the camp, and he called it the tent of meeting. And everyone who sought the LORD would go out to the tent of meeting, which was outside the camp. Whenever Moses went out to the tent, all the people would rise up, and each would stand at his tent door, and watch Moses until he had gone into the tent. When Moses entered the tent, the pillar of cloud would descend and stand at the entrance of the tent, and the LORD would speak with Moses.

Following their deliverance from Egyptian slavery, Israel the nation traversed into the Sinai Peninsula and camped around the mountain where Moses first met the Lord (cf. previous devotional). Though Moses re-ascended the mount to secure additional revelation, an impatient populace soon went off the rails. A golden calf enflamed their adulterous worship until Moses returned with executionary judgment. Exodus 32 finds Moses pleading with the LORD not to give up on His people, nor His promises.

Architectural plans already defined where people could approach God; namely, the Tabernacle (cf. Ex. 26), itself frequently called "the tent of meeting." Inside exterior canvas walls were courts, sacred furniture, and both the Holy Place and the Holy of Holies. With sacrificial blood, a priest could meet with God in the inner tent (cf. Lev. 16, Heb. 9:3-5), atoning for a nation's sins.

Interestingly, Exodus 33 speaks of a unique-to-Moses tent-of-meeting, outside the encampment of the tribes, separate from the Tabernacle. There, God and Moses talked as gazing outsiders looked on. As the divine Pillar descended, people stood in their entryways, aware, anticipating, wondering what God would discuss and disclose with a servant who shared His heart. Like you?

Questions:

Where's my tent-of-meeting with God? A place where His presence descends, His voice speaks, His ears hear?

Thoughts:

Prayer:

For establishing a "tent" for speaking and listening to God...

Psalm 5:3
O LORD, in the morning you hear my voice; in the morning...

"Does God Make My Day?"
Journal Summary Week 3

*What key truths did the Spirit of God impress
on my heart and life in this past week?*

Day 15 *Friendship with God - Genesis 22:10-12*

Day 16 *Acting without Consulting God - Genesis 25:29-34*

Day 17 *Grappling with God - Exodus 32:24-32*

Day 18 *Meeting the Burning Bush God 1 - Exodus 3:1-5*

Day 19 Meeting the Burning Bush God 2 - Exodus 3:4-6

Day 20 Meeting the Burning Bush God 3 - Exodus 3:6-12

Day 21 In the Tent of Meeting 1 - Exodus 33:7-9

In what way has the Lord urged me to change, or obey, this week?

In the Tent of Meeting - 2

Exodus 33:9-11

When Moses entered the tent, the pillar of cloud would descend and stand at the entrance of the tent, and the LORD would speak with Moses. And when all the people saw the pillar of cloud standing at the entrance of the tent, all the people would rise up and worship, each at his tent door. Thus the LORD used to speak to Moses face to face, as a man speaks to his friend. When Moses turned again into the camp, his assistant Joshua the son of Nun, a young man, would not depart from the tent.

Friendship, C.S. Lewis observed, is one of the four loves (also *affection, eros,* and *charity,* cf. <u>The Four Loves</u>).

"*[It]…arises when two or more companions discover that they have in common some insight or interest or even taste which the others do not share… it is when two such persons discover one another, when, whether with immense difficulties and semi-articulate fumblings, or with what would seem to us amazing and elliptical speed, they share their vision. It is then that Friendship is born*" *(pp.96-97).*

Do you find it amazing that God seeks friends among human beings? Enoch walked with God, no doubt in friendship. Abraham came to be God's friend through trusting and obeying God (James 2:23b), even when it was challenging, difficult, faith-stretching. Jesus told his disciples, "Not only servants, I call you friends" (John 15:15). Let it sink in – God desires a true friendship with you.

Moses and God had a common vision, to bring God's people into the land promised to Abraham, Isaac, and Jacob. A good land, one "flowing with milk and honey." To provide that leadership, Moses needed God's coaching and God's ear. They unpacked as true friends. Interestingly, nearby, young Joshua was learning from his mentor how to nurture a personal, daily relationship with God himself.

Questions:

Am I willing to grow in a genuine friendship, through the Spirit, with God himself? What are the regular steps friends take to deepen their relationship?

Thoughts:

Prayer:

For deepening my friendship with God himself...

Psalm 25:14
The friendship of the LORD is for those who fear him,
and he makes known to them his covenant.

Exodus 33:12-15

Moses said to the LORD, "See, you say to me, 'Bring up this people,' but you have not let me know whom you will send with me. Yet you have said, 'I know you by name, and you have also found favor in my sight.' Now therefore, if I have found favor in your sight, please show me now your ways, that I may know you in order to find favor in your sight. Consider too that this nation is your people."
And He said, "My presence will go with you, and I will give you rest." And he said to Him, "If your presence will not go with me, do not bring us up from here."

Guilt-stricken in sin, Adam hid in foliage *from* the presence of God. By contrast, desperate for helping empowerment, Moses plead in the tent *for* the presence of God. There is an "I need to be sure!" insistence pressing through Moses' tone. He had no interest trying to lead 2 million people into what God has promised by merely marshalling his own, human and inadequate resources.

His begging powerfully instructs us. "You say you know me, Lord. You say I have your favor. If so, show me now YOUR ways. I want to KNOW you (i.e., thoroughly, as if to say, "I require full alignment with You, Lord!"). This is YOUR people, Lord." The Lord assures, "My presence will go with you…", but Moses presses in. "If YOU are not going with me, I don't want to go anywhere!"

A remarkably dependent posture of Moses shines here. He realizes what Jesus would later remind us, "Without Me, you can do nothing" (Jn. 15:5b). Dare we attempt anything—studying, working, loving a spouse, parenting, handling finances, decision-making—apart from time with God? Time in which we say to Him, "If Your presence and ways are not in this, I can't go forward!"

Question:

Do I ask God-daily-for His ways and presence in the important callings I have in my life (work, family, relationships)?

Thoughts:

Prayer:

For discerning God's ways and presence in my callings...

Deuteronomy 26:17
You have declared today that the LORD is your God,
and that you will walk in His ways

Exodus 34:29-30, 34-35

When Moses came down from Mount Sinai…he did not know that the skin of his face shone because he had been talking with God. Aaron and all the people of Israel saw Moses, and behold the skin of his face shone…Whenever Moses went in before the LORD to speak with him, he would remove the veil, until he came out. And when he came out and told the people of Israel what he was commanded, the people of Israel would see the face of Moses, that the skin of Moses' face was shining. And Moses would put the veil over his face again, until he went in to speak with Him.

The glory of God can indeed transform the way a person looks. It can empower when a person shares what he/she hears from God. Jesus looked very normal to those who followed Him until…well, until those moments on a mountain in Galilee.

Matt. 17:2 And Jesus was transfigured before them, and his face shone like the sun, and his clothes became white as light.

Wow! Really?

Undoubtedly, God so uniquely brightened Moses' face so that the people would have visible assurance that Moses had been with God, that what Moses was saying was indeed from God. Paul tells us that Moses veiled his face when with the people, after sharing God's commands, so that they would not see the shining gradually dimming. Only face-to-face time with God could renew the glory.

Paul also tells us that today, "we all" are invited into this enlightening tent.

2 Cor. 3:18 We all, with unveiled face, beholding the glory of the Lord, are being transformed into the same image, from one degree of glory to another. For this comes from the Lord, who is the Spirit.

Wow! Really? Time beholding God's glory, taking in His revelation, face-to-face, can transform me into His image? Yes, yes indeed.

Questions:

As you spend time with God, do you sense a degree-by-degree brightening of your life? Being transformed, as a sunrise, into Jesus' likeness?

Thoughts:

Prayer:

For an eagerness to be face-to-face with God...

Psalm 3:3
But you, O LORD, are a shield about me,
my glory, and the lifter of my head.

Joshua 1:7-8

Only be strong and very courageous, being careful to do according to all the law that Moses my servant commanded you. Do not turn from it to the right hand or to the left, that you may have good success wherever you go. This Book of the Law shall not depart from your mouth, but you shall meditate on it day and night, so that you may be careful to do according to all that is written in it. For then you will make your way prosperous, and then you will have good success.

For many years, a younger Joshua attended at the elbow of Moses. As Moses' assistant (Ex. 24:13, Num. 11:28), he would shadow Israel's leader on Mount Sinai, organize troops for battle, hover around the tent of meeting, update Moses on developments among the tribes. Joshua fearlessly joined Caleb pleading with Israel to courageously obey, to eschew any fear, despite the spies' faithless report (Num. 14:16). Moses groomed him as Israel's next-gen leader (Dt. 1:38).

Now, at center stage, with Moses' obituary ringing in his ears (Josh. 1:2), Joshua's moment for true leadership chimed. Leadership demands strength; it also longs for success. Perhaps aged 60, standing before anxious millions grouped in tribes and family units, his example and guiding hand would make or break the future of God's people.

The Lord also desired a rise of confidence through Joshua. So He imparted how consistent victory could be realized, day by day, week by week, month by month, year after year. "Spend the time. Talk the book. Ponder the Laws. Understand their meaning. Press in on personal application. Never short-cut obedience. *For then you will make your way prosperous; then you will have good success.*

Talk about a formula with a Divine guarantee. God's "if...then(s)" must never be ignored. They promise so much and deliver even more for those with courage to spend time with God. Moments to take His word seriously.

Question:

Does the Word of God inhabit my mind, my mouth?

Thoughts:

Prayer:

For my success to be in knowing/keeping God's Word...

Psalm 119:57
The LORD is my portion; I promise to keep Your words.

Joshua 1:5, 9

No man shall be able to stand before you all the days of your life. Just as I was with Moses, so I will be with you. I will not leave you or forsake you.

"Have I not commanded you? Be strong and courageous. Do not be frightened, and do not be dismayed, for the LORD your God is with you wherever you go."

Should you be reading this during a stretch of life free from much challenge or care, you may be inclined to yawn. But for those of you who are facing genuine high-hurdles, you may just want to lean in.

What are those hurdles for you? Do you have anyone's life in your hands these days—your kids for example? What's your awareness level that your leadership in their lives, for good or for ill, will likely determine their future? And can you pull the kind of leadership and influence they need on you own? Or, are you influencing a department, a business, an organization? As a team member, or perhaps as the leader, do you sense others out of step with you because of your commitment to being God's woman or man in that role? How are you going to thrive (not just survive) in your spot? Again, can you pull it off on your own?

You can dig around the Biblical background sources to better appreciate the full extent of Joshua's challenge as he stood on the far side of the Jordan River. Yeah, with 2 million wondering what to do next and needing a home. On the other bank, pagan warriors by the thousands in scores of fortified cities eager to take you, your wife and kids, and your nation "out" as soon as you dare cross over. It's you or them. Where will Joshua find sufficient confidence to take his people across?

Needed: God's very presence. God's clear promise. The unseen God of Joshua's fathers to be his strength and courage in all the battles to come, whenever and wherever they might arise. You too?

Question:

Am I meeting and regularly talking with God enough to stay assured and confident in His presence, His promises, His help over every coming hurdle?

Thoughts:

Prayer:

For confidence in the Lord's supply of promise, presence, help...

Psalm 62:2
He alone is my rock and my salvation, my fortress;
I shall not be greatly shaken.

Joshua 8:30-35

At that time Joshua built an altar to the LORD, the God of Israel, on Mount Ebal,
...And they offered on it burnt offerings to the LORD and sacrificed peace offerings. And there, in the presence of the people of Israel, he wrote on the stones a copy of the law of Moses, which he had written. And all Israel, sojourner as well as native born, with their elders and officers and their judges, stood on opposite sides of the ark...just as Moses the servant of the Lord had commanded at the first, to bless the people of Israel. And afterward Joshua read all the words of the law, the blessing and the curse, according to all that is written in the Book of the Law. There was not a word of all that Moses commanded that Joshua did not read before all the assembly of Israel, and the women, and the little ones, and the sojourners who lived among them.

Under Joshua's obedient leadership, Israel not only crossed the Jordan River successfully (at flooding time), but also began defeating the Canaanite cities and armies in impressive fashion. That is until Ai. Because of one soldier's disobedient sin (Achan, cf. 7:20-21), 3 dozen Israeli soldiers lay dead on the battlefield. Joshua was distraught. Achan confessed and was executed. God's blessing returned, and soon Ai joined the list of defeated cities.

Still, Joshua wasn't satisfied. Notice the first words of the passage, "At that time..." Joshua knew Israel was guaranteed victory IF they fully obeyed God's word; and utter defeat IF they chose independent, selfish acts of disobedience. On a key mountain, Joshua builds an altar, asking the priests to lead the nation in sacrificial worship. And... this leader *takes the time* to write the Law of Moses on flat stones (we're talking Exodus and Leviticus!)...and then also *takes the time* to read "all that is written in the book of the Law" to the people. "There was not a word that Moses commanded that Joshua did not read" to EVERYONE! They all stood before the Lord and listened to the Lord. Impressive...to say the least. And a tremendous investment in their future.

Question:

Am I meeting and regularly talking with God enough to stay assured and confident in His presence, His promises, His help over every coming hurdle?

Thoughts:

Prayer:

For giving God and His word central focus in my family...

Proverbs 7:1
My son, keep my words, treasure up
my commandments with you.

Commitment to God and His Word

Joshua 23:14 & 24:24-26

"And now I am about to go the way of all the earth, and you know in your hearts and souls, all of you, that not one word has failed of all the good things that the LORD your God promised concerning you. All have come to pass for you; not one of them has failed."

The people said to Joshua, "The LORD our God we will serve, and his voice we will obey." So Joshua made a covenant with the people that day, and put in place statutes and rules for them at Shechem. And Joshua wrote these words in the Book of the Law of God. And he took a large stone and set it up there under the terebinth that was by the sanctuary of the LORD.

The bookends of Joshua's life signal the key to Joshua's success in all the years that spanned between. As a young attendant to Moses, Joshua witnessed how weighty the words of God, inscribed in stone tablets, were to Moses. How central they were to be to the life and prosperity of God's people. When Moses died, God assured Joshua success if "this book of the Law" did not depart from his mouth. If he would "meditate on it day and night." Then "he would have success and then he would make his way prosperous.

Now, as life this side of glory ebbs, Joshua resolutely restates the utter reliability, and the ongoing significance of the statutes, rules, and words in the Book of the Law of God. To forsake, or even forget, God's word was to invite both personal and national disaster. Once more, before drawing his last breath, Joshua wanted to hear Israel say, "We will listen to God's voice; we will obey His word."

N.T. Wright declared,

> "The Bible is the book of my life. It's the book I live with, the book I live by, the book I want to die by."

So it was with Joshua. With you? It was God's presence and God's Word that brought great confidence, courage, capacity for leadership, and an accomplishment of the will of God. Know God. Read the Word. Take time every day to make a portion of it your daily compass.

Question:

Am I meeting and regularly talking with God enough to stay assured and confident in His presence, His promises, His help over every coming hurdle?

Thoughts:

Prayer:

For a life-long commitment to meeting God in His Word...

Psalm 119:97
I love Your Law; it is my meditation all the day.

"Does God Make My Day?"
Journal Summary Week 4

What key truths did the Spirit of God impress
on my heart and life in this past week?

Day 22   In the Tent of Meeting 2 - Exodus 33:9-11

Day 23   In the Tent of Meeting 3 - Exodus 33:12-15

Day 24   In the Tent of Meeting 4 - Exodus 34:29-30, 34-35

Day 25   Success from Careful Obedience - Joshua 1:7-8

Day 26 Courage from God's Presence - Joshua 1:5, 9

Day 27 Time With the Word of God - Joshua 8:30-35

Day 28 Commitment to God and His Word - Joshua 23:14, 24:24-26

In what way has the Lord urged me to change, or obey, this week?

Tuned In To the Calling of God

1 Samuel 3:10-13

And the LORD came and stood, calling as at other times, "Samuel! Samuel!" And Samuel said, "Speak, for your servant hears." Then the LORD said to Samuel, "Behold, I am about to do a thing in Israel at which the two ears of everyone who hears it will tingle. On that day I will fulfill against Eli all that I have spoken concerning his house, from beginning to end. And I declare to him that I am about to punish his house forever, for the iniquity that he knew, because his sons were blaspheming God, and he did not restrain them.

Scripture quite often chides men for not *truly* listening. When people do nothing with what they hear from God, their capacity for listening diminishes. "Be doers of the Word," James presses, "and not merely hearers who delude themselves."

In this chapter, Samuel is a boy serving in the priestly house of Eli. Eli and his two biological sons (Hophni & Phineas) had ignored God's word and God's voice for so long that God halted further attempts at tuning them in. Still, God had something He wanted to say to His leaders and his people He needed a set of ears that would do more than just take in information. Samuel's heart was ready.

Years later, it's clear that Samuel never forgot the wonder, the joy, and the importance of clearly hearing the voice of the Lord. Through repeated times of interaction, Samuel and God were on face-to-face terms with each other, not unlike Moses' experience. God entrusts His word with those who will obey it, regardless of how difficult carrying through with obedience might be.

To be sure, today, you and I are also invited to have ears tuned to God's calling, to His voice and speaking into our life situations. Shall we not echo Samuel's eager reply, "Speak, for your servant hears!"? Music to God's ears!

Questions:

God can wake us up that we might listen. Are you eager and prepared to respond to His voice as did Samuel? Why not make it a habit?

Thoughts:

Prayer:

For God to clearly speak my name for His purpose...

Psalm 18:6
From his temple he heard my voice,
my cry to him reached his ears.

71

Delighting In the Lord's Law

Psalm 1

Blessed is the man who walks not in the counsel of the wicked, nor stands in the way of sinners, nor sits in the seat of scoffers; but his delight is in the law of the LORD, and on his law he meditates day and night. He is like a tree planted by streams of water that yields its fruit in its season, and its leaf does not wither. In all that he does, he prospers. The wicked are not so, but are like chaff that the wind drives away. Therefore the wicked will not stand in the judgment, nor sinners in the congregation of the righteous; for the LORD knows the way of the righteous, but the way of the wicked will perish.

If you're a reader, I wonder, what is your habit when a new book lands in your hands. Do you skip ahead right off to Chapter 1, or do you take a moment to read the "Introduction"? A good introduction provides the reader a couple of things. One is a well-stated (and compelling) reason to bother reading the next 200 pages (sometimes stated as a question). Another is the key argument, or point, of the book--a claim critical for living life with success and joy. Sometimes, an introduction will also offer the supporting ideas which substantiate the case being made.

Psalm 1 is exactly this—the "introduction" to the Book of the Psalms. It directly answers "Why bother spending time with God in the Psalms?" Reason: living in the fullness of God's happy blessing. Key argument: *Whom* you spend time with *will determine* both your life and your end. Either being "tree-like" (rooted, watered, blessed, fruitful, destined to stand) vs. being "chaff" (wind-driven, sinning, wicked, destined to perish).

With whom will you spend your time? The Lord, His Word, and others owning a similar passion for a blessed life...or the wicked, the sinners, the scoffers. The latter crowd will simply destroy your heart and life. The Lord, however, will always refresh you with streams of living water, knowing your way, blessing your steps.

Questions:

When's the last time I took stock of those with whom I'm spending heart-shaping time? Are there any adjustments needed? Enough time with Him?

Thoughts:

Prayer:

For spending time meditating on the Lord/His Word...

Colossians 3:16
Let the word of Christ dwell in you richly...

Morning Pleading With the Lord

Psalm 5:1-3, 7-8

Give ear to my words, O LORD; consider my groaning.
Give attention to the sound of my cry, my King and my
God, for to you do I pray. O LORD, in the morning you
hear my voice; in the morning I prepare a sacrifice for
you and watch. But I, through the abundance of your
steadfast love, will enter your house. I will bow down
toward your holy temple in the fear of you. Lead me, O
Lord, in your righteousness because of my enemies;
make your way straight before me.

Do you have enemies? They come in all sizes and shapes. Some of our
most formidable enemies we can't see – the spiritually wicked forces
in high places Paul references in Ephesians 6:12. Put on available
armor for the battles they stir up (vvs. 13-17). Yet other enemies sit
next to us at the office, attend family gatherings, or work behind-
the-scenes to make sure you are not considered for the promotion.

While some enemies may be imagined, even self-created (and we
ought to be willing to de-construct these), real enemies can cause
sleepless nights. Inward groaning. Crying and cries. We fall to sleep
worrying; we wake wondering if God is fully aware of "my situation."
Having to face everyday enemies ought motivate urgent help-
seeking. We require a fresh perspective which settles, a calming we
can't quite muster up on our own. Only God's wisdom will do. Perhaps
an Advocate (cf. Rom. 8:26, Heb. 4:16-18) to supply what can make
the difference.

The Psalter often echoes with pressing pleas for help with
threatening, destructive enemies. Entering "God's house" such
pleading is a good thing. Your Lord's steadfast love opens wide the
door; your commitment to "righteousness" (i.e., doing what is right
regardless of what your enemy does) provides His straight path to
follow (cf. Jesus, Matt. 5:43-44). Cry and groan in God's presence.
His Son did. His children have the same access. You have a listening
and answering Helper.

Questions:

What are the enemies I'm facing? Am I entering "God's house" to secure His perspective and provision? Any "treatment of enemy" directives I am being called to obey?

Thoughts:

Prayer:

For seeking God's presence and power in facing enemies...

Luke 6:27 (Jesus)
"Love your enemies, do good to those who hate you..."

Psalm 15

O LORD, who shall sojourn in Your tent? Who shall dwell on Your holy hill? He who walks blamelessly and does what is right and speaks truth in his heart; who does not slander with his tongue and does no evil to his neighbor, nor takes up a reproach against his friend; in whose eyes a vile person is despised, but who honors those who fear the LORD; who swears to his own hurt and does not change; who does not put out his money at interest and does not take a bribe against the innocent. He who does these things shall never be moved.

Is life about the journey or the destination? This songful reflection encompasses both. Traveling with God down the wandering pathway. Dwelling with God in His exalted abode. The point? Who truly enjoys the benefit of living, now and forever, in relational companionship with God himself?

Surprisingly, not the person who flawlessly fulfills exacting religious rituals. Rather, the person whose passionate habit is to live out integrity, such that others recognize and benefit from it. Derek Kidner (Psalm 1-72, p. 81) neatly summarizes the answer of the verses.

> "His character: true. His words: restrained. His allegiance: clear cut. His dealings: honorable. His place: assured…the qualities the Psalm describes are those that God creates in man, not those He finds in him."

James echoes the Psalm's final promise.

> "Be doers of the word, not hearers only…a doer who acts will be blessed in his doing" (1:22, 25).

Insecurity and instability plague the too-easily "moved" person; once here, then there. Shifting standards. Opportunistic allegiances. One posture today, another tomorrow.

To exhibit God's character fulfills. To experience God's companionship unleashes genuine joy. Today, tomorrow, and for all the morrows to come. Draw near to God and He too will draw near with intent: to create new character within (cf. 2 Pet. 1:4).

Question:

How might I use this Psalm to inspire my choices, and shape my character, to grow in companionship with the Lord?

Thoughts:

Prayer:

For seeking God's presence and power in facing enemies...

Isaiah 33:15-16
He who walks righteously...will dwell on the heights.

Setting the Lord Before Me

Psalm 16:7-8

I bless the LORD who gives me counsel;
in the night also my heart instructs me.
I have set the LORD always before me;
because He is at my right hand, I shall not be shaken
(i.e., moved).

We are not used to saying it that way. By "it" I mean describing someone in THE most influential, critical place in my life. For an infant, a committed mother and a father. For an athlete, a great coach. For someone battling cancer, an insightful physician. What examples might you cite? And, who is your most important person? Whoever it is, he or she IS "at your right hand."

Yet in middle-eastern culture, the description meant even more. To "be at the right hand" was to be in the place of honor, privilege, access. After his crucifixion, Jesus ascended, exalted as seated at His Father's right hand. "At the left hand" wasn't far behind. James' and John's mother prematurely asked if her boys could be seated, "one on the left and one on the right" when Jesus came into his glory.

When you read the Scripture above (again), put these two "right hand" aspects together and consider how you operate. Listen to the Psalmist. His life was about insisting that the Lord's presence permeate His moments. Counsel at night. Setting the Lord before him 24-7. Making sure God is constantly in the most influential place and in the most honored place of whatever goes on with him.

Proverbs 3 "In all your ways acknowledge Him..."

Note the outcome: *I shall not be shaken* (or moved). There's nothing cool in Hebrew parlance about getting moved and shuffled around. Successful life required rootedness, stability, solid, sure footing. It depends on your right hand.

Question:
What am I doing, practically, to put the Lord at my "right hand"?

Thoughts:

Prayer:
To more consistently put God in THE place of influence...

Psalm 21:7
...through the steadfast love of the Most High
he shall not be moved.

Seeking God In His Word

Psalm 119:10-11, 15-16

With my whole heart I seek You; let me not wander from Your commandments! I have stored up Your word in my heart, that I might not sin against You.

I will meditate on Your precepts and fix my eyes on Your ways. I will delight in Your statutes; I will not forget Your word.

The longest chapter in the Bible is Psalm 119. It hosts 176 verses. It sits in the very middle of the Bible. And, the whole of it is about one subject: *the unique, unparalleled importance of the Word of God.* An apologetic for the Book itself.

Yep, it's long. But, it is well worth reading all the way through. Believe it or not, it was actually written to be memorized. Each of the 22 sections (8 verses each) starts with a successive letter of the Hebrew alphabet (i.e., "A" starts the first line of Psalm 119:1, "B" stars the first line of Psalm 119:9, and so on).

So the question arises. Why would anyone memorize these 22 sections of 8 verses? Answer—to never forget ALL the benefits of knowing God, hearing God, following God, gaining instruction from God, having a heart, mind, will shaped by God ARE TO BE HAD through attention to the Word of God. To never neglect pursuing all God has for us from Himself in His Word. "All Scripture is breathed out by God," Paul reminded Timothy, "and thus it is profitable..." (2 Timothy 3:16).

The verses above are just a sample of the Psalm's feast. But notice it is not a Book we are out to know. It's a Person. Eight times in 4 verses, it's about "You" or "Your" (i.e., God). This is not an academic pursuit; this is a relationship journey. The Psalmist, like Paul, is saying, "I want to know Him." To seek Him. To think like Him. To hate sin like Him. To live in His ways and delight His heart. Wow! What an incredible opportunity when the Word of my God renews the center of my heart.

Questions:

Am I memorizing portions of God's Word? Will I? Start with...?

Thoughts:

Prayer:

For falling in love with God and His Word...

Psalm 119:172
My tongue will sing of your word...your commandments are right.

Daniel 6:10-11

When Daniel knew that the document had been signed, he went to his house where he had windows in his upper chamber open toward Jerusalem. He got down on his knees three times a day and prayed and gave thanks before his God, as he had done previously. Then these men came by agreement and found Daniel making petition and plea before his God.

For decades, he flawlessly served Babylon, the previous empire and its ruler, Nebuchadnezzar. Remarkably Daniel, a Jewish exile, not only survived when the Persians took over, he thrived. Yet King Cyrus, a.k.a. Darius, arrogant in his conquests, revealed a vulnerability to companions eager to discredit this relic.

They knew their king was prideful, and they knew Daniel was prayerful. Why not pit Daniel's praying against their sovereign's arrogance? "O King! Unite your new kingdom! All petitions and all prayers should be laid at your feet, and no where else. Let any disobedience mean death." Quickly, foolishly, Cyrus agreed with the stroke of a pen, a blanket edict without any possible revocation.

More important to Daniel than a human ordinance was being in God's presence three times a day. Scholar Joyce Baldwin (Daniel) notes,

"Windows...open toward Jerusalem...3 times a day [reflects] Psalm 55:17-18 where David testifies to the value of set habits of prayer. The rabbis attributed the practice to Moses."

As he had done previously, this courageous leader determined to do continuously. Centuries later, Peter with John echoed, "Whether it is right in the sight of God to listen to you rather than to God, you must judge..." (Acts 4).

God Himself loved His daily appointments with his servant, so much so that He honored His servant's commitment. Daniel slept peacefully with lions while a restless Cyrus tossed and turned with the consequences of reckless rule making.

Question:
Lord God, do you and I meet during each day, regularly, without fail?

Thoughts:

Prayer:
To refuse any compromise in meeting daily with God...

Psalm 55:16
But I will call to God, and He will save me,
evening and morning and at noon

"Does God Make My Day?"
Journal Summary Week 5

What key truths did the Spirit of God impress
on my heart and life in this past week?

Day 29 Tuned in to the Calling of God - 1 Samuel 3:10-13

Day 30 Delighting in God's Law - Psalm 1

Day 31 Morning Pleading with the Lord - Psalm 5:1-3, 7-8

Day 32 Sojourning, Dwelling with the Lord - Psalm 15

Day 33 *Setting the Lord Before Me - Psalm 16:7-8*

Day 34 *Seeking God in His Word - Psalm 119:10-11, 15-16*

Day 35 *Prioritizing Time with God - Daniel 6:10-11*

In what way has the Lord urged me to change, or obey, this week?

Living By Every Word Of God

Matthew 4:1-4

Then Jesus was led up by the Spirit into the wilderness to be tempted by the devil. And, after fasting forty days and forty nights, he was hungry. And the tempter came and said to him, "If you are the Son of God, command these stones to become loaves of bread." But he answered, "It is written, 'Man shall not live by bread alone, but by every word that comes from the mouth of God'."

To drive outside of Jerusalem east and south, into the Judean desert, is to encounter arid terrain covered with countless rocks of every shape and size. Had Jesus said the word, a million or more could have suddenly become so many loaves in a bakery as large as the mind might imagine.

Famished, why not? Yes, the suggestion came from the tempter, but what was wrong with it? If extended solitude coupled with personal deprivation had raised any self-doubt about who he was, or even why he found himself in such desperate straits, a creative miracle might well reset his mind, bring refreshment to the body. He surely *could* erase the weakness, take charge of his diminishing condition. After all, he was the Son of God.

Yet the Savior refused to act merely out of what his own mind reasoned, or out of what his flesh was demanding. He desired to *truly* live, not just physically exist. "I need something more than bread," he replied. "I need whatever word comes from my Father's mouth." He remembered that his ancestors had desperately wandered in a desert. That His Father "humbled" them and "let [them] go hungry" and fed them with day-by-day manna (cf. Deut. 8:3) to learn the same lesson. True nourishment is living obediently to what one hears from the Father day-by-day, even when reason and flesh demand otherwise.

Question:

I eat every day. Am I listening every day for the nourishment of God's voice, God's words, God's direction?

Thoughts:

Prayer:

For eager humility to listen daily to God's voice...

Deuteronomy 8:20
...so shall you perish, not obeying the voice of the Lord your God.

In Secret With the Father

Matthew 6:1, 5-6

"Beware of practicing your righteousness before other people in order to be seen by them...

And when you pray, you must not be like the hypocrites. For they love to stand and pray in the synagogues and at the street corners that they may be seen by others. Truly I say to you, they have received their reward. But when you pray, go into your room and shut the door, and pray to your Father who is in secret. And your Father who sees in secret will reward you."

Biblically tutored Christians understand at least two truths about righteousness.

Truth one is that those who chose to trust Christ as their Savior, by faith, are given the permanent gift of Christ's own righteousness. "He made him who knew no sin to be sin for us, that we might become the righteousness of God in him" (2 Cor. 5:21). This righteousness is "imputed," credited to our account. We cannot earn it; it is endowed. Our Father, who declares our "justification," sees us in Christ as righteous. Have you so trusted Christ for this unique gift?

A second truth is that we, standing by faith in grace and credited with righteousness, are called to express righteousness as a lifestyle. More simply, we can live "rightly," in a way that demonstrates what has been credited to us. This is what Jesus speaks of above when saying "Beware of *practicing your righteousness*...". The Lord's command is simple. Don't publicly parade "right living" in order to be commended or celebrated by men. Hypocrites love the stage, craving applause. Whatever reward attaches to this is already dispensed.

Time with God is not about public performance. You'll find your Father in an unpopulated room with your name on it. He's there, eager to hear from you there, ready to respond to you there. So the hymn, "Take time to be holy, speak oft with thy Lord, much time spent in secret, with Jesus alone."

Questions:

Am I growing in my honesty with God when I meet in secret with my Father? How can I more naturally speak with Him in childlike eagerness?

Thoughts:

Prayer:

For meeting daily with my Father in secret...

Psalm 7:10
My shield is with God, who saves the upright in heart.

Mark 1:35-39

And rising very early in the morning, while it was still dark, he departed and went out to a desolate place, and there he prayed. And Simon and those who were with him searched for him, and they found him and said to him, "Everyone is looking for you." And he said to them, "Let us go on to the next towns, that I may preach there also, for that is why I came out." And he went throughout all Galilee, preaching in their synagogues and casting out demons.

In the press of life, someone else always needs something more. Any servant may repeatedly "burn the candle at both ends." Even Jesus. Mark 1:34 indicates his yesterday was long –

"at sundown, they brought all who were sick and oppressed by demons. The whole city gathered at the door, and he healed many who were sick...he cast out many demons."

Reflect on this. Surrounded relentlessly by sickness and demonic spiritual powers. How quickly did sleep come when finally the Savior's head hit the pillow?

An internal alarm roused Jesus. A mission moved him through pre-dawn darkness to a secret place, known alone to him and His Father. Critical soul-restoring minutes, perhaps hours. Might we wonder what Jesus needed more, shut-eye or sustaining prayer? What do we need more, despite the chorus of demands? For the God-man, first things deserve first place. Time with God before time with men. Otherwise, time with men forfeits direction from God.

How instructive this short report! Peter's frustration bubbles up, as if saying, "How dare you be unavailable!" [Notice...to those who have already heard about you.] But Jesus received directing vision. On to unreached towns. On to isolated people. Good news needs spreading, exposure, chances to hear and receive by faith. A passion expanding the scope of ministry.

Questions:

How sacred is my commitment to securing pre-dawn refreshment and direction from the Father, through the Spirit? To insist the urgent not crowd out the important?

Thoughts:

Prayer:

For prioritizing time with God over life's demands...

Proverbs 4:7
The beginning of wisdom is this: get wisdom, get insight.

Expectantly In God's Presence

Luke 2:36-38

And there was a prophetess, Anna, the daughter of Phanuel, of the tribe of Asher. She was advanced in years, having lived with her husband seven years from when she was a virgin, and then as a widow until she was eighty-four. She did not depart from the temple, worshiping with fasting and prayer night and day. And coming up at that very hour she began to give thanks to God and to speak of him to all who were waiting for the redemption of Jerusalem.

Alone for 60 years, yet not alone. One could easily speculate how Anna felt when her husband of but 7 years suddenly died. Luke provides little detail. Widows were frequently forgotten, neglected, uncared for, bereft of support. Vulnerable, powerless, often taken advantage of. Apparently there was no brother to step in and raise up offspring for Anna's husband's name. Thus no children. She lived mostly alone for 60 years.

But, apparently, not alone. Somewhere in that six decade stretch, she began a habit of hanging around Jerusalem's majestic temple. She learned to worship. She discovered fasting sharpened her awareness of God's presence. She found herself praying the Psalms, perhaps even reading and reciting the Prophets. Anna became consumed in begging God for the redemption of David's city. For God to fulfill what the Prophets promised…though quite aware of the unholy alliance between the Priests and the Politicians. Were her prayers useless?

She had been in God's presence daily, an unnoticed nobody daring to plead once again, and yet again, with the Almighty for the arrival of redemption. Her cry, "Perhaps today?" And then…she saw an infant boy, especially blessed by Simeon. God, in whose presence she lived, finally said "Here, my daughter…take a good look. And, spread the word."

Questions:

Do I find that my time with God increases my eagerness for God to fulfill His promises? Does it ready me to share the good news about Christ?

Thoughts:

Prayer:

For a greater concentration on the Lord when in His presence...

Colossians 4:2
Continue steadfastly in prayer,
being watchful in it with thanksgiving.

Choosing the Good Portion

Luke 10:38-42

Now as they went on their way, Jesus entered a village. And a woman named Martha welcomed him into her house. And she had a sister called Mary, who sat at the Lord's feet and listened to his teaching. But Martha was distracted with much serving. And she went up to him and said, "Lord, do you not care that my sister has left me to serve alone? Tell her then to help me." But the Lord answered her, "Martha, Martha, you are anxious and troubled about many things, but one thing is necessary. Mary has chosen the good portion, which will not be taken away from her."

Let's face it. It is very difficult for *doers* to slow down. Doers thrive on multi-tasking (though, interestingly, recent studies show multitasking diminishes the quality of any one of the tasks). They also feel affirmed when their *busy-ness* reputation is both demonstrated (again!) and duly applauded (though they readily demur the praise). Doers assume that everything depends on their maximum effort. Getting the job done is job one.

Enter Martha the "doer," and her sister Mary, also a doer, yet less intensely so. When Jesus and friends came for dinner, it was clearly a two-sister job, at least as Martha sized it up. Mary sized the same opportunity up differently; personal time with Jesus was rarefied air. Listening to Jesus rather than serving Jesus was Mary's Job One.

So…who was right? Some side with the over-wrought Martha. But not Jesus. He (no doubt kindly, yet) firmly corrected the one who was "trying to make sure everything was right." Busy serving that produces anxiousness, stressing over secondary details, should be set aside. "One thing is necessary," Jesus continued. "Mary has chosen it, the 'good' that she will never lose." Listening well to Jesus, even midst the busiest press of life, is always Job One.

Question:
Am I allowing my busyness to keep me from Job One?

Thoughts:

Prayer:
For prioritizing time listening to Christ...

Philippians 4:6
Do not be anxious about anything, but in everything
by prayer and supplication with thanksgiving
let your requests be made known to God.

Life-Changing Time With God

Luke 19:1-10

Jesus entered Jericho and was passing through. And there was a man named Zacchaeus. He was a chief tax collector and was rich. And he was seeking to see who Jesus was, but on account of the crowd he could not, because he was small in stature. So he ran on ahead and climbed up into a sycamore tree to see him, for he was about to pass that way. And when Jesus came to the place, he looked up and said to him, "Zacchaeus, hurry and come down, for I must stay at your house today." So he hurried and came down and received him joyfully. And when they saw it, they all grumbled, "He has gone in to be the guest of a man who is a sinner." And Zacchaeus stood and said to the Lord, "Behold, Lord, the half of my goods I give to the poor. And if I have defrauded anyone of anything, I restore it fourfold." And Jesus said to him, "Today salvation has come to this house, since he also is a son of Abraham. For the Son of Man came to seek and to save the lost."

So what was it? Was he merely "passing through" Jericho, or did he intend all along to eventually hang at Zacchaeus' place? If Luke's larger account is at all chronological, Jesus has already underscored God's approval of a humbled, repentant "tax-harvester" (i.e., collector, cf. Luke 18:9f). Man sees the outward appearance; God sees the heart.

Curious but wanting to keep his distance, Zacchaeus finds a sycamore-limb perch to steal a look. His Savior—soon to be Lord— owns a different agenda. "I *must* TODAY stay at your house," Jesus surprises. Luke's reporting notes divine necessity in Jesus' declaration. Not satisfied with a wave from afar, Jesus wants time with us in whatever we call home. His goals are clear. Extend grace. Establish relationship. Change quietly, from the inside out. Transform into living like sons of Abraham, who was God's wonderful friend (cf. James 2:23b).

96

Questions:

Do I want more than just a distant view and relationship with Jesus? If so, in what ways has He "come to stay" at my house?

Thoughts:

Prayer:

For the Lord Jesus to come and stay with me...

Isaiah 41:8
But you...whom I have chosen,
the offspring of Abraham, my friend.

John 1:38-40, 43-46

Jesus turned and saw them following and said to them, "What are you seeking?" And they said to him, "Rabbi" (which means Teacher), "where are you staying?" He said to them, "Come and you will see." So they came and saw where he was staying, and they stayed with him that day, for it was about the tenth hour. One of the two who heard John speak and followed Jesus was Andrew, Simon Peter's brother. The next day Jesus decided to go to Galilee. He found Philip and said to him, "Follow me." Now Philip was from Bethsaida, the city of Andrew and Peter. Philip found Nathanael and said to him, "We have found him of whom Moses in the Law and also the prophets wrote, Jesus of Nazareth, the son of Joseph." Nathanael said to him, "Can anything good come out of Nazareth?" Philip said to him, "Come and see."

In the introductory verses of his Gospel, John reveals what God the Son, the Word, came to do. Remarkably, to "explain" Him (i.e., to make God known, 1:18). No one has ever seen God. Yet Jesus invited, "Come and see."

The Nazarene introduces men to God the way we get to know each other. Pick-up basketball. A coffee shop hour. "Come on over for dessert." "I've got two tickets to the game." Helping someone move into a new apartment.

Sure, an "extra" was in play in the above verses. These career fishermen were wondering if Jesus was in fact the long awaited Jewish Messiah. And, camel-skin covered John was pointing the finger his way. But it was early. Proof would unfold over the next 36 months. Jesus would have to overcome the conventional wisdom that no one important ever came from the disregarded village of Nazareth.

The truth is that these men would never be fully convinced without following Him: without spending time and watching and doing what He was training them to do. They would learn who He truly was in team moments, a thousand or more of them. In the hours of interaction and challenge, in faith-stretching episodes, in moments of unparalleled wonder. The God-man kept urging, "Come, and see."

Question:

Am I getting to know Jesus in the specifics of everyday life?

Thoughts:

Prayer:

Of response to Jesus' "come and see" invitation...

Mark 1:17 (Jesus)
"Follow Me, and I will make you become fishers of men."

99

"Does God Make My Day?"
Journal Summary Week 6

Day 36 *Living by Every Word of God - Matthew 4:1-4*

Day 37 *In Secret with the Father - Matthew 6:1, 5-6*

Day 38 *Early Mornings with God - Mark 1:35-39*

Day 39 *Expectantly in God's Presence - Luke 2:36-38*

Day 40 *Choosing the Good Portion - Luke 10:38-42*

Day 41 *Life-Changing Time with God - Luke 19:1-10*

Day 42 *Time with Jesus - John 1:38-40, 43-46*

In what way has the Lord urged me to change, or obey, this week?

Following Jesus Anywhere

John 4:39-42

Many Samaritans from that town believed in him because of the woman's testimony, "He told me all that I ever did." So when the Samaritans came to him, they asked him to stay with them, and he stayed there two days. And many more believed because of his word. They said to the woman, "It is no longer because of what you said that we believe, for we have heard for ourselves, and we know that this is indeed the Savior of the world." After the two days he departed for Galilee.

She went to the well again. At noon. The least desirable *and* least embarrassing time to go. Avoid the local traffic, the disapproving glances. She could simply get her water and get back to experiment number six, who provided a roof but not a covenantal promise. She arrived to find the watering hole crowded with but one other, a Jewish stranger.

With nothing but a depleted, unsatisfying life, how could she have ever imagined the Savior of the world was sitting there, anxious to spend time *with her*? It was, he explained, his "food." Even more, how could she imagine that she would soon run back through her neighborhood shouting, openly thankful the Savior had both exposed her shame and given her a grace-filled drink of living water?

All in Samaria. Unthinkable! The place well-spoken Jews never frequent. With people whom well-regarded Jews never contact. With a woman whom a well-respected rabbi should never talk. Her simple faith response, coupled with her boundless joy, woke up her sleepy village. More living water flowed, more faith, more joy. And, this Savior stayed longer. Time invested to explain God, and to mentor surprised disciples to see how ready the harvest truly was.

Following Jesus, you find yourself with people who simply do not understand that it is not about religion. It is about relationship with God. Days spent with the Savior…and offering grace-filled drinks of living water.

Question:

Am I learning from the Savior to truly see the harvest about me?

Thoughts:

Prayer:

To follow Jesus to places and people I've avoided...

---

2 Corinthians 5:14, 16
Christ's love controls us…we regard no one merely by the flesh.

Abiding In the Vine

John 15:1-5

I am the true vine, and my Father is the vinedresser.
Every branch in me that does not bear fruit he takes
away, and every branch that does bear fruit he prunes,
that it may bear more fruit. Already you are clean
because of the word that I have spoken to you. Abide
in me, and I in you. As the branch cannot bear fruit by
itself, unless it abides in the vine, neither can you,
unless you abide in me. I am the vine; you are the
branches. Whoever abides in me and I in him, he it is
that bears much fruit, for apart from me you can do
nothing.

Sheldon Vanauken and his wife, Davy, were not Christians as he
began his journey through Oxford University. Yet in God's providence,
they would meet a unique scholar, Clive Staples (C.S.) Lewis, who
mentored them toward faith. Later, Sheldon would lose Davy in
an untimely death, and mourn her deeply. Yet his faith held firm.
His experience with fellow Christians led him to this observation
(A Severe Mercy):

> *"The best argument for Christianity is Christians: their joy, their
> certainty, their completeness.*
>
> *But the strongest argument against Christianity is also
> Christians—when they are somber and joyless, when they are
> self-righteous and smug in complacent consecration, when they
> are narrow and repressive....then Christianity dies a thousand
> deaths."*

Jesus shared a key life-truth with his disciples; namely, that even
though He would be physically absent from them during the next era
on the Kingdom time-line, they and He could stay vitally connected.
Indeed, staying vitally connected would be the key to everything
truly important in life. An "abiding" disciple is a fruit-laden branch of
Jesus, full of His joy, His peace, His purpose, His life.

Connected vitally to Him, we can do all things (cf. Phil. 4:13).
Detached we can do nothing.

Questions:
Am I staying connected, hour by hour, to the Vine? What are the small habits I can develop that keep the connectedness?

Thoughts:

Prayer:
To follow Jesus to places and people I've avoided...

John 16:24
Ask, and you will receive, that your joy may be full.

The Book of the Acts

All these with one accord were devoting themselves to prayer, together with the women and Mary the mother of Jesus, and his brothers (1:14)...

And they devoted themselves to the apostles' teaching and the fellowship, to the breaking of bread and the prayers (2:42)...

And when they had appointed elders for them in every church, with prayer and fasting they committed them to the Lord in whom they had believed (14:23).

The great reformer Martin Luther (1483-1546) is to have said,

"As it is the business of tailors to make clothes and of cobblers to mend shoes, so it is the business of Christians to pray."

It may well be that a reading in the book of Acts prompted such a claim. Early Christians prayed. When Jesus ascended, they went to Jerusalem to pray and wait for what God was sending (i.e., the promised Holy Spirit). When 3,000 people responded in faith to the Peter's gospel, they gathered themselves in smaller groups, and devoted themselves to (among other things) prayer. Even before his salvation, Cornelius habitually prayed and God was listening (Acts 10). When new churches were established, leaders were carefully chosen and dedicated with serious, extended prayer.

It is the business of Christians to pray. How about you? Is it your business?

Abraham Lincoln confessed,

"I have been driven many times to my knees by the overwhelming conviction that I had nowhere else to go. My own wisdom, and that of all about me, seemed insufficient for the day."

If the early Christians' business was to pray, if our greatest President was often driven to his knees, if we have access to the very heart and presence of God because of Jesus (Acts 4:16-18), give God a chance to make your day...every day. Pray. Pray again. Pray often. Pray always. Pray as if your life depended on it, for it does.

Questions:

Am I praying? Am I praying with my spouse? My kids? My friends?

Thoughts:

Prayer:

To make it "my business" to pray...

Acts 10:31
"Cornelius, your prayer…has been heard by God."

107

1 Corinthians 2:11-13

For who knows a person's thoughts except the spirit of that person, which is in him? So also no one comprehends the thoughts of God except the Spirit of God. Now we have received not the spirit of the world, but the Spirit who is from God, that we might understand the things freely given us by God. And we impart this in words not taught by human wisdom but taught by the Spirit, interpreting spiritual truths to those who are spiritual.

We may not fully appreciate the reality of our limitations. Regardless, researchers know we humans can perceive only 30% of the range of the sun's light and 1/70 of the spectrum of electromagnetic energy. Other animals exceed those abilities. Bats detect insects by sonar; pigeons navigate by magnetic fields; bloodhounds perceive a world of smell unavailable to us.

How great the gap, then, between our thoughts and the thoughts of a God whose knowledge and wisdom knows no limit. His "omniscience" means God knows all things actual and possible. "My thoughts," God reveals, "are not your thoughts; My ways are not your ways. For as the heavens are higher than the earth, so are my ways higher than your ways and my thoughts than your thoughts" (Is. 55:8-9).

Given our limitations rooted in our creaturely humanness, what chance do we have at accurately understanding anything about God? The truth? We have a tremendous chance because of the Holy Spirit, who

- is God (one of the 3 Persons of the Triune God)
- knows exhaustively the thoughts of God
- reveals accurately to us in ways we can understand
- provides truth about the things freely given to us by God
- uses spiritually gifted people to teach others spiritual truths

Question:

What sources, precious Spirit, have you placed in-and-around my life from which I can understand the thoughts and ways of God, if I give You time?

Thoughts:

Prayer:

To deepen and invest in understanding what God freely provides...

Proverbs 2:4-5
Search as for hidden treasures...
you will find the knowledge of God.

Transformed By the Word/Spirit of God

2 Corinthians 3:15-18

Yes, to this day whenever Moses is read a veil lies over their hearts. But when one turns to the Lord, the veil is removed. Now the Lord is the Spirit, and where the Spirit of the Lord is, there is freedom. And we all, with unveiled face, beholding the glory of the Lord, are being transformed into the same image from one degree of glory to another. For this comes from the Lord who is the Spirit.

Ever had this experience? You watch a movie with someone, only later to talk about it. Over a cup of joe you inquire, "What was, do you think, the point of the movie?" The answer you hear surprises. "Were we watching the same flick?" you ask. "I didn't get that at all." Honestly, this happens all the time. Depending on our personal "filters," different people can read the same article or watch the same movie and come away with widely disparate thoughts and conclusions.

The Apostle Paul encountered this over and over. Reading the Old Testament to his Jewish friends, he noticed how they seemed unable to find it pointing to Christ...at all! Like a veil covered their eyes; blind to Jesus in Scripture. Yet when Paul read the Old Testament, all of it pointed to Jesus, the remarkable Messiah from Nazareth (cf. Luke 24:25-27).

This, of course, explains so much. If your non-Christian friends and/ or family get nothing from reading the Bible—and you get so much! —it's because you as Jesus' disciple have had the veil of spiritual blindness removed from your "eyes." When you read and reflect on Scripture, you have the priceless opportunity to "behold the glory of the Lord," even to be transformed in those moments into His likeness. All because the Spirit uses the word of God to increasingly change us, degree by degree becoming like our Savior and Lord. "We all" are invited to behold.

Question:

Good Father, can I not find more time even in the press of my days, to reflect on your word and be, day-by-day, transformed into Your likeness?

Thoughts:

Prayer:

To take advantage of "unveiled" time with the Lord...

1 Thessalonians 5:23
May the God of peace himself sanctify you completely...

Equipped By God to Stand Firm

Ephesians 6:13-17

Therefore take up the whole armor of God, that you may be able to withstand in the evil day, and having done all, to stand firm. Stand therefore, having fastened on the belt of truth, and having put on the breastplate of righteousness, and, as shoes for your feet, having put on the readiness given by the gospel of peace. In all circumstances take up the shield of faith, with which you can extinguish all the flaming darts of the evil one; and take the helmet of salvation, and the sword of the Spirit, which is the word of God,

Soldiers readily understand these verses. We non-combatants, not so much. Today's modern warrior carries at least 60 lbs. of gear, up to 90 lbs. The base uniform, gloves, boots, glasses, body armor protecting the side, groin, collar, the helmet, his/her weapon, ammo. Add a gear-filled rucksack, plus electronics, batteries, and the list goes on (we haven't mentioned chemical protection gear). Needing to strike the balance between sufficient protection and being overburdened, soldiers need to fight, stand, survive, prevail. It's life or death.

Today's Christians often head into daily battle unarmed and flippantly unprotected. Gear is provided; we simply neglect to suit up. Yet one can hardly miss our orders. "*Take up* the whole armor of God." When strapped on, "you may be able to withstand (survive <u>and</u> prevail) in the evil day." Paul is confident that any believer can stand firm when the truth of God holds together (as with a belt) all the equipment. That a commitment to righteous living can shield the vital organs. That the gospel which puts us at peace with God provides boots for tromping through any battle. Solid faith can extinguish arrows lobbed in with destroying fire. Knowing we are rescued (saved) and will be rescued protects our minds. Using the Spirit's Word—a nimble weapon—for close infighting with a pressing enemy.

Gear up! Think about God's truth, live rightly, handle attacks with faith, square up with stable footing embedded in the truth of the gospel. Think and fight with confidently memorized, applied Scripture. Gear up, every day! It's life or death.

Question:

When is the last time I had a good conversation with spiritual companions about what our gear is and how to best use it?

Thoughts:

Prayer:

To put on more consistently God's armor...

Romans 16:20
The God of peace will soon crush Satan under your feet.

Longing to Truly Know Christ

Philippians 3:8-10

Indeed, I count everything as loss because of the surpassing worth of knowing Christ Jesus my Lord. For his sake I have suffered the loss of all things and count them as rubbish, in order that I may gain Christ and be found in him, not having a righteousness of my own that comes from the law, but that which comes through faith in Christ, the righteousness from God that depends on faith—that I may know him and the power of his resurrection, and may share his sufferings, becoming like him in his death,

Katrina, Harvey, Irma, Maria. Just a few of the scores of recent hurricane names. Year 2017 witnessed 17 major storms including some 10 hurricanes. So many storms we forget which came when. The National Hurricane Center began naming Atlantic storms in 1953.

What is not so easily forgotten is how much unimaginable loss occurs when such violent systems explode in a populated region. People often lose everything. Seemingly worse are the losses incinerated through wind-whipped wild fires. So often, absolutely nothing remains save piles of ash.

The loss of all things. So frequently, so understandably, viewed as a "negative." Yet not always. Paul the Apostle ("sent one") indicates that his total loss was not only necessary, but ultimately advantageous. His life's resume included an impressive array of personal, professional (mostly religious) accomplishments. However, as long as Paul clung to them, he would miss life's most important opportunity; namely, to gain Christ. To be found in Him. To have a given (not earned) righteousness not of his own, but the true righteousness available ONLY through faith in Christ. To KNOW Christ, both in His power and in His suffering.

To know the Lord Jesus Christ in every way, in every portion and part of one's life is worth the loss of anything else. Such losses score an eternal win.

Question:

Father God, to know well your Son in every area of my life, what are those things (attitudes, personal pride areas) that need to be lost?

Thoughts:

Prayer:

To know Christ in every way...

1 John 2:4
Whoever says "I know Him" but does not keep His
commandments is a liar, and the truth is not in him,

115

"Does God Make My Day?"
Journal Summary Week 7

Day 43 *Following Jesus Anywhere - John 3:39-42*

Day 44 *Abiding In the Vine - John 15:1-5*

Day 45 *Time in Prayer with Your Father - The Book of Acts*

Day 46 *Time with the Thoughts of God - 1 Corinthians 2:11-13*

Day 47   Transformed by the Word/Spirit of God - 2 Corinthians 3:16-18

Day 48   Equipped by God to Stand Firm - Ephesians 6:13-17

Day 49   Longing to Truly Know Christ - Philippians 3:8-10

In what way has the Lord urged me to change, or obey, this week?

The Word Indwelling Richly

Colossians 3:16-17

Let the word of Christ dwell in you richly, teaching and admonishing one another in all wisdom, singing psalms and hymns and spiritual songs, with thankfulness in your hearts to God. And whatever you do, in word or deed, do everything in the name of the Lord Jesus, giving thanks to God the Father through Him.

Should someone, sometime, ask you what the Bible is all about, how would you answer? How might you summarize the point of the Bible? Paul's letter to these early believers in Colossae (a city in what is today the country of Turkey) offers a simple summary. Using it, you might say, "The Bible is the Word of (or *about*) Christ." Jesus dared to claim on several occasions that all of Scripture points to and speaks of Him.

In these verses, the apostle is urging that all the disciples in the Colossae church should nurture an eager, increasingly-familiar intimacy with the Scriptures, which point to Christ, speak about Christ, present His life and example and teaching, and instruct us on how He Himself can life in us and through us by the Holy Spirit. If the "word of Christ" dwells in each of us and among us all in a "rich" way, what will be the result?

All kinds of important and life-enriching realities. We will be free to offer—and receive—both positive teaching and admonishing correction. Readily exchanging God's wisdom. What's more, we'll worship with song and scripture, while deepening in thankfulness. Our entire living—what we say, what we do—will flow out of the prioritized presence of God's Word in our lives.

Some Christians today live just this way. Humbly, freshly in the richness of minds and hearts fully enriched by God's presence bestowed by God's Word.

Questions:

Lord Jesus, how might the richness of Your Word be more fully invested in my life? Might memorizing Scriptures be a key step?

Thoughts:

Prayer:

For more of the richness of the Word of Christ...

John 6:68 (Peter)
"Lord, to whom might we go?
You alone have the words of eternal life."

Receiving the Word Well

1 Thessalonians 2:13

And we also thank God constantly for this, that when you received the word of God, which you heard from us, you accepted it not as the word of men but as what it really is, the word of God, which is at work in you believers.

With every passing year, with each month and week, indeed with each unfolding day, more comes "at us." Messages of every kinds: radio, television, yard signs, lectures and speeches, "breaking news," sales promotions, social media, podcasts, tweets, emails, new apps which deliver messages and images, advertisements, billboards, direct mail appeals, robo-phone calls. What have I missed? The tsunami is as relentless as anything we experience in living.

The challenge is two-fold. On the one hand, the important task of *selectivity*. I will choose to take in what, and why? What will I read? I will watch what? What will I listen to? Dwell on (i.e., entertain more than once)? One who desires to be open-minded should nonetheless exercise care. An open mind can simply become a collection of garbage, not unlike an open sewer. Few would want the precious resource of their minds to filled with pollution.

The second challenge is *responsiveness*. That is, what will I do with what I take in? This largely depends on sorting out, from what one has encountered, what is truthful and what is not to be trusted. What to believe and what to reject. What information merits internalization and action.

When reading Paul's letters to Thessalonia (new believers living in the upper region of what we today call Greece), one senses his love for these fresh disciples. They responded to "the Word." Given grace to recognize that what they were hearing from Paul and his ministry companions was not just another "also ran" message from human speculation. Rather, they were hearing the Word of God *through* men. And, it was at work *in* them, changing them day by day. Such is the power of God's living revelation when it is recognized, received, and given its opportunity in us.

Question:
Will I let you, guiding Holy Spirit, direct what I take in and do with what I receive?

Thoughts:

Prayer:
For what I invest in my heart and mind...

1 Thessalonians 4:1
"As you received from us how to please God....do so more..."

In His Presence Forever

1 Thessalonians 4:13-18

But we do not want you to be uninformed, brothers, about those who are asleep, that you may not grieve as others do who have no hope. For since we believe that Jesus died and rose again, even so, through Jesus, God will bring with him those who have fallen asleep. For this we declare to you by a word from the Lord, that we who are alive, who are left until the coming of the Lord, will not precede those who have fallen asleep. For the Lord himself will descend from heaven with a cry of command, with the voice of an archangel, and with the sound of the trumpet of God. And the dead in Christ will rise first. Then we who are alive, who are left, will be caught up together with them in the clouds to meet the Lord in the air, and so we will always be with the Lord. Therefore encourage one another with these words.

For those who "love His appearing" (cf. 2 Timothy 4:8), the current silence is deafening. Within the family—around the expansive body of Christ—there is little anticipating conversation about the return of the Lord Jesus Christ.

Yes, the topic can be found in any number of evangelical doctrinal statements. But if (as Francis Chan suggests) the 3rd person of the Trinity (i.e., the Holy Spirit) is yet today "the forgotten God," the imminent return of the Lord Jesus Christ is the forgotten hope. Whom do you find looking up on a daily basis? Whom do you hear regularly praying, "Come, Lord Jesus!" (cf. Revelation 22:20).

The upward set of my heart was determined early. The probable, sudden, and largely unexpected return of the Lord Jesus dropped me to prayerful knees when I was nine. I needed forgiveness, and I didn't want to be left behind. Clear, Spirit-empowered Sunday-night-service preaching couldn't have made it clearer. A few years later, when my aging grandfather lived in the corner bedroom of our home, I slipped in one day to find him reading the 1st Thessalonians passage. He had me read it with him, finishing with tears, 'Ah, Davy...'dat will be a great day!"

What *will* make that day great? So much. Nine words capture the best part: *and so we will always be with the Lord.* Are you ready? Are you daily looking up?

Question:
Lord Jesus, will you teach me to keep my daily focus upward?

Thoughts:

Prayer:
Anticipating all that Jesus will bring when he returns...

Revelation 22:20
He who testifies to these things says,
"Surely I am coming soon."

Sound Teaching Discarded

1 Timothy 4:1-5

Now the Spirit expressly says that in later times some will depart from the faith by devoting themselves to deceitful spirits and teachings of demons, through the insincerity of liars whose consciences are seared, who forbid marriage and require abstinence from foods that God created to be received with thanksgiving by those who believe and know the truth. For everything God created is good, and nothing is to be rejected if it is received with thanksgiving, for it is made holy by the word of God and prayer.

"We BELIEVE!" The play-offs in American sports often generate a sea of such signs, flags, and banners waved by a rabid, eager fan base. The more who have faith, the greater the chances for the team's success. Or so it is believed. Even when crushing losses happen in crucial games, die-hards still...believe.

Beliefs can be tenaciously held, but they also can be surrendered. "I don't believe that anymore," someone admits. "I used to. My parents believe that way. And I did for a while. But not now." Of course, it's one thing to change from being a "Cub fan" to a "Cards fan." It's another thing to switch one's spiritual allegiance and core philosophical convictions. The former may cost the price of changing out a logo cap and sweatshirt. But the latter has eternal consequences. Even destructive consequences.

It may surprise, and it surely should sober, to understand that those who have believed and walked in the truth can take a major wrong turn. The Holy Spirit's word is, "Don't be surprised." It happens, and it will happen more as our current age heads into its final stages. The dark side of the spiritual world offers powerful, attractive (mostly prohibitive) substitutes for what God's Word teaches. Stay Biblical and stay positive. Receive all that God gives you thankfully.

Question:

In this world of competing ideas (substitute beliefs contrary to the Word) are there any deceptions tempting me away from Christ/the Word?

Thoughts:

Prayer:

For discernment and steadiness in my faith...

1 Timothy 6:10
For the love of money is a root of all kinds of evil. It is through this craving that some had wandered away from the faith...

A Life Shaped By the Word

2 Timothy 3:14-17

But as for you, continue in what you have learned and have firmly believed, knowing from whom you learned it and how from childhood you have been acquainted with the sacred writings, which are able to make you wise for salvation through faith in Christ Jesus.

All Scripture is breathed out by God and profitable for teaching, for reproof, for correction, and for training in righteousness, that the man of God may be complete, equipped for every good work.

Some parents make it a priority. Other parents do not. Timothy came from a home that didn't, and did.

From indicators that are less-than-complete, Timothy's non-Jewish father was, most likely, dispassionate about religion and faith. Yet dad was just one side of the equation. On the other side were a Jewish grandmother (Lois) and mother (Eunice), women not only of quiet, powerful faith, but disciples who saw to it (cf. 2 Timothy 1:5) that young Timothy knew, understood, and believed the Scriptures. His faith flowered early, watered by their faithful praying, grounded in the soil of supernatural revelation. "From childhood…acquainted with the sacred writings….able to make you wise for salvation through faith in Christ Jesus."

So much about the centrality of Scripture for the developing heart. Neglectful parents starve their children's souls when Scripture is not honored, read, and discussed at home. You cannot reap when nothing is sown. Conversely, intentional parents find ways to read Scripture together as a family and weave Scripture into the ebb 'n' flow of everyday living. Our personal worth to God is clarified by Scripture. The way we conduct relationships. How we communicate with one another (at home and on the street) are shaped by Scripture. The values portrayed through movies and popular culture evaluated with Scripture.

Why? Because nothing else equals the value of Scripture, because of the Source of Scripture. Because nothing else written must have such a comprehensive influence on every part of our life. Because what God has said has the power to shape any and every person into a man or woman of God.

Question:

God, will I give you the opportunity–consistently and each day–to make my day with your life-shaping "breath," the very word of God?

Thoughts:

Prayer:

For making interaction with Scripture a must-do...

Psalm 119:24
Your testimonies are my delight…my counselors.

Bring the Parchments

2 Timothy 4:9-13

Do your best to come to me soon. For Demas, in love with this present world, has deserted me and gone to Thessalonica. Crescens has gone to Galatia,Titus to Dalmatia. Luke alone is with me. Get Mark and bring him with you, for he is very useful to me for ministry. Tychicus I have sent to Ephesus. When you come, bring the cloak that I left with Carpus at Troas, also the books, and above all the parchments.

About some Scripture we wonder, "These things are so personal, so time-bound; why include such things for us today?" What value are personal notes about Paul's companions and travel? A left-behind coat, books, parchments?

In reality, these Scriptures reveal instructive aspects of the walk with God through real life relationships, through disappointments and loyalties, in decisions, changing circumstances, in things which anchor hearts despite storms.

Consider the likely backstories. Paul is arrested a 2nd time by Roman authorities, a second Roman incarceration. This time a release is unlikely, the life and death stakes are higher. Some of Paul's companions desert under the pressure; he is increasingly alone at the very time he needs encouragement. Others leave to strengthen Christian fellowships elsewhere. Crescens' encouragement was needed in Galatia. Titus to those in Dalmatia. Yet Luke, a physician, attends to Paul's physical *and* companionship needs.

Timothy is to bring Mark—a young man who failed Paul's mission on his first assignment. Now he has proven himself, and Paul needs him for ministry in Rome. Also, "bring the cloak…the books…and above all the parchments." Arrested individuals often had their 2nd cloak taken from them. Anticipating this when taken in Troas, Paul likely hid it with friends, along with precious materials. The parchments, likely copies of Paul's favorite Scriptures, now requested, that Paul might spend his final days with God in His Word.

Question:

Father, I need your presence in all of my life's details. How can I see Your hand and provision in Your people around me, and in Your Word?

Thoughts:

Prayer:

For looking for God's presence and provision in difficulty...

Hebrews 10:25
...encouraging one another, and all the more
as you see the Day drawing near.

2 Timothy 4:16-18

At my first defense no one came to stand by me, but all deserted me. May it not be charged against them! But the Lord stood by me and strengthened me, so that through me the message might be fully proclaimed and all the Gentiles might hear it. So I was rescued from the lion's mouth. The Lord will rescue me from every evil deed and bring me safely into his heavenly kingdom. To him be the glory forever and ever. Amen.

He was wrongly accused of multiple murders, despite a provable alibi, a successful polygraph, and no credible forensic evidence. Officials willfully ignored facts. Convicted, he spent nearly 30 years in solitary confinement awaiting execution on Alabama's death row. Fifty-four men walked by him to the execution chamber.

Sustaining Anthony Ray Hinton through long years was a childhood friend, visiting faithfully over some 1,560 weeks. It took 14 years of contested litigation before the Supreme Court, in a rare unanimous ruling, released Hinton on April 3, 2015. His lawyer, Bryan Stevenson, writes that Hinton's story is "something of a miracle. [His journey coursed] around the gates death...[a man] who nonetheless remains hopeful, forgiving, and faithful" (*The Sun Does Shine*, St. Martin's Press, 2018).

History finds the human story profusely littered with such justice miscarriage. Most notable, that of Jesus the Christ. Completely innocent, yet brutalized unto death as if the worst of the worst. His chosen apostles enduring a similar end. God's sons and daughters may find themselves—in the will of God—the target of wrongful accusation, arrest, execution. And along the way, desertion by others.

Soak in Paul's perspective. Forgiveness: "May it not be charged against them" (i.e., their desertion of Paul). Comfort: "But the Lord stood by me and strengthened me." Purpose: "That through me the message (i.e., the Gospel) be fully proclaimed...that all might hear it." In our tough, alone moments, directed by our Father's will, may we simply be empowered by our Lord's sweet presence.

Question:

Few spots are tougher than "aloneness." How can I recognize your presence with me, precious Lord, when going solo in difficult times?

Thoughts:

Prayer:

For God's presence in alone times...

Romans 12:14
Bless those who persecute you; bless and do not curse them.

"Does God Make My Day?"
Journal Summary Week 8

What key truths did the Spirit of God impress
on my heart and life in this past week?

Day 50   The Word Indwelling Richly - Colossians 3:16-17

Day 51   Receiving the Word Well - 1 Thessalonians 2:13

Day 52   In His Presence Forever - 1 Thessalonians 4:13-18

Day 53   Sound Teaching Discarded - 1 Timothy 4:1-5

Day 54   *A Life Shaped by the Word - 2 Timothy 3:14-17*

Day 55   *Bring the Parchments - 2 Timothy 4:9-13*

Day 56   *God's Unique Presence in Trial - 2 Timothy 4:16-18*

In what way has the Lord urged me to change, or obey, this week?

God's Word, God's Presence

Hebrews 4:11-13

Let us therefore strive to enter that rest, so that no one may fall by the same sort of disobedience. For the word of God is living and active, sharper than any two-edged sword, piercing to the division of soul and of spirit, of joints and of marrow, and discerning the thoughts and intentions of the heart. And no creature is hidden from his sight, but all are naked and exposed to the eyes of him to whom we must give account.

In Privilege the Text, Abraham Kuruvilla notes,

> "...this ancient text (i.e., Scripture) must be preached to an audience in a manner that yields application to change lives for the glory of God...[understanding] Scripture as the *viva vox Dei* (living voice of God)."

The author of the N.T. book of Hebrews believes this. Scripture is God's voice, living, active, sharp, probing and discerning, surgical and healing. When listening to Scripture we are in God's presence, and He in ours. Fully disclosed to God, He eagerly urges excellence. As we reject disobedience and eschew quitting, He coaches us forward. That we might enter a future "rest" promised to those who run with endurance and finish well.

As the passage warns, some in Jesus nonetheless fall short. Like some in Israel, believing Yahweh was God yet still refusing to live obediently. At critical junctures, refusing to trust God, unfaithfulness resulted in loss of significant blessing and reward. God's presence dishonored as God's voice is disobeyed.

A pastor noted, "An F16 fighter jet is an amazing aircraft with incredible capabilities. But there is one thing that a jet pilot requires above all else. That the aircraft reacts completely to his control. If it were to have 'a mind of its own' regardless of how remarkable that might sound, it would end up doing as much flying as a door stop. In the same vein, even if we had all the gifting under the sun, God as the ultimate 'pilot' of our lives, will only do amazing and remarkable things with our lives if we are fully under His control."

Question:

Father, any part of my living that is not aligned in obedience to Your Word, a dishonor to Your presence?

Thoughts:

Prayer:

For a tenacious commitment to obedience...

Acts 5:29
Peter and the apostles answered,
"We must obey God rather than men."

The Father's Presence In Discipline

Hebrews 12:5b-10

My son, do not regard lightly the discipline of the Lord...
It is for discipline that you have to endure.
God is treating you as sons. For what son is there whom
his father does not discipline? If you are left without
discipline, in which all have participated, then you are
illegitimate children and not sons. Besides this, we have
had earthly fathers who disciplined us and we respected
them. Shall we not much more be subject to the Father
of spirits and live? For they disciplined us for a short
time as it seemed best to them, but He disciplines us
for our good, that we may share His holiness.

According to www.fatherhood.org, "there is a father absence crisis in America. 20 million children—more than 1 in 4—live without a father in the home. So what? Such kids are 4X more likely to end in poverty, 7X more likely to become pregnant as a teen, more likely to have behavioral problems, to abuse drugs and alcohol, more likely to commit crime and land in prison.

Kids by the millions sense they are illegitimate. Dad is absent, along with his discipline. It's fundamentally disorienting, creating a gaping hole in one's identity. Good dads understand that personal, thoughtful, character-shaping discipline is one of the most powerful expressions of fatherly-love. It demonstrates he cares, anchoring the heart. Good dads value sons and daughters. They prayerfully guide, challenge, correct, forge, and eventually launch into the world Christ-centered influencers. A developing young person longs for the presence of his/her father, hungers for his attentive discipline.

Hebrews 12 affirms all this for each of us who are in Christ, and more. Our earthly fathers' discipline prepares us for the perfect, soul-forging shaping of our Heavenly Father. Our part is to "not lightly regard" the Lord's discipline. Solomon's *Proverbs* resound with urgent pleas for youth to both pursue wisdom as treasure, to receive instruction/discipline with eagerness. Only fools rebelliously arch their backs.

Whatever your Father is doing these days to discipline your insides, welcome it. His presence is uniquely in what is happening with you, and He deeply loves you enough to share His life-sustaining Holiness with you, His Son, His daughter.

Question:
Good Father, what part of my life needs to grow in your Holiness?

Thoughts:

Prayer:
To more fully share in my Father's holiness...

1 Peter 1:15
As He who called you is holy, you also be holy in all your conduct

Our Overseeing Shepherd's Nearness

1 Peter 2:21-25

For to this you have been called, because Christ also suffered for you, leaving you an example, so that you might follow in his steps. He committed no sin, neither was deceit found in his mouth. When he was reviled, he did not revile in return; when he suffered, he did not threaten, but continued entrusting himself to him who judges justly. He himself bore our sins in his body on the tree, that we might die to sin and live to righteousness. By his wounds you have been healed. For you were straying like sheep, but have now returned to the Shepherd and Overseer of your souls.

No one welcomes mistreatment. Few would choose to live in a state of enslavement if any chance of obtaining one's personal freedom were possible. Yet a good number of early Christians were slaves. Rome looked for 500,000 additional slaves annually to meet the manpower needs of the empire. As the opportunity for Christian faith was offered, a good number of those enslaved trusted Christ.

Believing slaves were "free in Christ" and "equal heirs" of God in the Church, but their position in society-at-large remained the same. Not a few were in less-than-encouraging situations, oft subjected to personal suffering. Not surprisingly they wondered if God would rescue them, or at least bring some longed-for relief.

Prompted by the Holy Spirit, Peter sets a different frame around their circumstances.

"Your suffering is a divine calling; your situation is being managed by God's care; your responses can be that of your Savior's."

Peter dares to suggest that the unjust treatment and suffering can bring redemption and healing change into the lives of others.

What's more, there is a Shepherd who oversees your life, even in its most difficult episodes. His promises assure that we are being led purposefully into a future of rest and joy with Him. The Good Shepherd promised, "Behold, I am with you always." Thus David sang, "The Lord himself is my Shepherd; I shall never be in want."

Question:
Good Shepherd, how well am I doing in understanding that tough stretches are part of your calling in my life?

Thoughts:

Prayer:
To follow my Shepherd wherever He leads...

Psalm 23:2
He leads me beside quiet waters; He restores my soul.

1 John 1:5-7

This is the message we have heard from him and proclaim to you, that God is light, and in him is no darkness at all. If we say we have fellowship with him while we walk in darkness, we lie and do not practice the truth. But if we walk in the light, as he is in the light, we have fellowship with one another, and the blood of Jesus his Son cleanses us from all sin.

Yes. You're right. We don't say it like that: "fellowship." We say, "Let's hang out." We tailgate, go to dinner, ball games, parties, concerts. We sit in coffee shops that look musty but feel cool. Around the fire pit. At the campsite. A weekend at the lake home, playing games, eating anything other than health food. No pressure. Small agendas. Whatever happens is refreshing.

Ninety-nine times out of hundred, we're with others for good times, for relational deepening. We share, learn to trust, keep secrets, offer encouragement, help each other when stuck. The Bible calls it *fellowship*. The Greek term, "koinonia," means all of these things: sharing, partaking, partnering, participating, associating. Deepening in relational life together with partners you trust. We come to both enjoy and count on someone's presence in our life.

Here's God's incredible offer. We can hang with Him, and He loves to hang with us. The opening verses of John's first letter to believers exclaims "we've seen and experienced God's Life – Jesus Christ the Son – which means we have *koinonia* with the Father and with His Son and with one another."

And yet there is a requirement. God doesn't do darkness. He loves people who are sinful. He does everything He can to reach and redeem them. But once redeemed, if you're going to hang with God, you can't "walk in darkness." Rather, we hang with God when we readily admit, confess, and shed our sin. God is light, and he shines with righteousness. And those who hang with Him do the same.

Question:

What remnants of "darkness" may be hindering my hang time with you, Lord Jesus?

Thoughts:

Prayer:

To honestly walk with God in His light...

Romans 6:13
Present the members (of your body)
as instruments of righteousness

Family Time With the Father

1 John 2:12-14

I am writing to you, little children, because your sins are forgiven for his name's sake. I am writing to you, fathers, because you know him who is from the beginning. I am writing to you, young men, because you have overcome the evil one. I write to you, children, because you know the Father. I write to you, fathers, because you know him who is from the beginning. I write to you, young men, because you are strong, and the word of God abides in you, and you have overcome the evil one.

You've already noticed the Apostle John's understanding of who makes up the family of our Heavenly Father. At least 3 generations: children, young men, fathers. Each generation has a different kind of relationship with the One who gave them birth and life.

Children are delightful and messy. Dennis and Barbara Rainey note that every child needs,

"Parents who don't freak out when their children are caught lying, stealing, hiding things, making stupid choices...and more" (The Art of Parenting).

Children realize they spill more, break more things, get dirtier more quickly than those who are older in the family. They need to know— over and over again—that they are forgiven by a Father who won't reject them because of their chaos.

Young men/women are eager to prove themselves against the odds. Desiring to pursue a passion, unsure but nonetheless confident, they need the Father's "go for it!" Personally, they have no interest in being a casualty. Spiritually, they need to experience—to learn to use—the conquering power of the Word over the threatening power of Satan.

Fathers? Great fathers have a proven track record of trusting God, of finding Him faithful through thick-and-thin. They are both rudders (direction) and ballast (stability) for God's family. They lead well because they *know* God the Father.

Question:

What generation, Lord, do I find myself in your family?

Thoughts:

Prayer:

To grow in the family of God...

---

1 John 3:1
See what kind of love the Father has given us...
children of God we are!

Guess Who's Interested In Dinner?

Revelation 3:19-20

Those whom I love, I reprove and discipline, so be zealous and repent. Behold, I stand at the door and knock. If anyone hears my voice and opens the door, I will come in to him and eat with him, and he with me.

The 2nd and 3rd chapters of the Revelation of Jesus Christ contain specific messages for 7 early churches in Asia Minor (today, Turkey). Each church in the world is a lampstand for the Lord Jesus. He cares about the condition of each, and for the believers of His Body. He cares enough to speak to them directly.

The 7th letter (Rev. 3:14-22) went to the church in Laodicea, a wealthy city in a fertile valley. Flush with an abundance of cash, luxurious clothing, the best health care. John Stott (What Christ Thinks of the Church, 1958) writes,

> *"The pride of Laodicea was infectious. Christians caught the plague... [believers] became smug and self-satisfied, and Jesus Christ needed to bluntly expose them...I need nothing, they said...they thought they were doing fine, but Christ described them as blind and naked beggars."*

Their spiritual complacency, a pervasive "half-heartedness," aroused the Lord Jesus' most pungent message, most penetrating diagnosis, most surprising reaction. These Christians were utterly distasteful to Him: "I will spit you out of my mouth!" he warns, if there is no repentance, no renewed fervency.

Yet grace appeals. "Listen, I stand at the door and knock," Jesus pleads. "If any one opens the door, we can begin again to dine." [Stott]...

> *"Our heart or soul is likened to a dwelling...the living Christ comes to visit. He now stands on our front doorstep and knocks. He wants to be admitted. It is a visit from the Lover of our soul. If we do open the door of our heart to Jesus Christ and let Him in, He will bring an end to our beggary. He will dine with us; we shall be permitted to dine with Him. The joy of the Christian life."*

Questions:

Is there complacency in my life, Lord Jesus, that arouses you?
Will I hear Your knock for renewed fellowship and refreshment?

Thoughts:

Prayer:

For restoration in spiritual fervency...

Revelation 3:21
To him who overcomes I will grant to sit with me on My throne.
(Jesus)

God's Dwelling Place Is With Men

Revelation 21:3-4

And I heard a loud voice from the throne saying, "Behold, the dwelling place of God is with man. He will dwell with them, and they will be his people, and God himself will be with them as their God. He will wipe away every tear from their eyes, and death shall be no more, neither shall there be mourning, nor crying, nor pain anymore, for the former things have passed away."

In 1880, Dwight Laymen Moody published a small volume entitled *Heaven*. Five years and almost 90,000 copies later, the original printing plates having worn thin, it was republished via newer technology ("electrotype plates") in Chicago. Six Chapters – Its Hope, Its Inhabitants, Its Happiness, Its Certainty, Its Riches, Its Rewards.

Moody writes,

> *If there is one word above another that will swing open the eternal gates, it is the name of Jesus. There are a great many pass-words and by-words down here, but that will be the countersign up above. Jesus Christ is the "Open Sesame" to heaven. Any one who tries to climb up some other way, is a thief and a robber. But when we get in, what a joy above every other joy we can think of,* **will it be to see Jesus Himself all the time, and to be with Him continually.** *Isaiah has given this promise of God to every one who is saved through faith: "Thine eyes shall see the King in His beauty; they shall behold the land that is very far off."*

Since the creation of the Garden and the first human family, God has longed to dwell with His people. His love driving Him to continually share the infinite joys of His indescribably beautiful fellowship. This dwelling-with-us will be the key feature of eternity, which can (and should!) begin today, and every day, until we feel his hand wiping the final tears from our eyes, now beholding Him in all His glory.

Question:

Are my hopeful eyes focused enough on the eternal day to come?

Thoughts:

Prayer:

To enjoy every foretaste of God's intimate presence now...

Revelation 22:17
The Spirit and the Bride say, "Come! Let him that hears come!"

"Does God Make My Day?"
Journal Summary Week 9

Day 57 *God's Word, God's Presence - Hebrews 4:11-13*

Day 58 *The Father's Presence in Discipline - Hebrews 12:6-10*

Day 59 *Our Overseeing Shepherd's Nearness - 1 Peter 2:21-25*

Day 60 *Walking in the Fellowship of Light - 1 John 1:5-7*

Day 61 Family Time with the Father - 1 John 2:12-14

Day 62 Guess Who's Interested in Dinner? - Revelation 3:20

Day 63 God's Dwelling Place is with Men - Revelation 21:3-4

In what way has the Lord urged me to change, or obey, this week?

Some Reflection On Experiencing His Presence

Perhaps those times when we truly, tangibly *experience* the *presence* of God are more rare. Many Christians – perhaps you – might admit feeling alone when "doing devotions." You sit, read, think a bit, pray for a minute or two, and yet come away wondering if you and the Lord actually invested time together. Were you both in the same room?

You have a lot of company. A relationship with God can frequently feel one-sided. But is this not especially the lot, I wonder, of those who believe one can simply pop-in and pop-out of God's presence, as if filling up your tank at a local gas station or dropping off a pile of clothes at a dry-cleaner? Why is it that we don't approach Him like we do a thorough work-out at the fitness center, or setting aside time for dinner with friends?

Is meeting with God, having Him "make your day," a brief appointment, or an anticipated encounter of candid unpacking and sharing hearts? Are we not too often guilty of attempting to have some brief time with the Lord of the Universe, too quickly wedged between other (more pressing) must-do's?

> *"Somewhere in the middle of 'The Messiah,' I was overwhelmed with the tangible presence of God."*

During a recent, hours-long drive across the Mid-west, with my spouse at the wheel, I was listening to George Frederick Handel's *The Messiah*. Two discs full of majestic music expressing the glory of the gospel. The message-laden compositions are repetitive, yet not at all annoying. They offer extended moments to consider and re-consider the weighty meaning of what God the Father did through sending the Messiah, God the Son. Somewhere in the middle of that presentation, I was overwhelmed with the tangible presence of God. My heart produced tears welling up, my soul freshly experiencing the truth and joy of God's goodness to me in Christ, and to Pamela and me as a couple. I had trouble handling the overflow of God's presence. When I regained some composure, I spoke to my bride of what had just happened. Not surprisingly, she immediately resonated with all I was trying to share.

Our encumbered lives do not willingly yield extra hours just to be with God. Revelation 3:20's picture of Jesus knocking and speaking through the door could, perhaps should, arrest our attention. "I'm willing, eager, to have dinner with you," the Lord Almighty invites. "Will you open the door?"

Slow down. Clear bigger chunks of the schedule. Establish a tent of meeting. Open the door. Listen to the voice of the Spirit in the Word, tumbled repeatedly in your mind. Behold the glory, and goodness, of your Savior. Worship. Be changed. Tear up. You are on a journey to a place where His presence will always be truly, tangibly experienced.

David A. Staff

Life Question Self-Evaluation

A life defined by following Christ in our mission:
Connecting people to life-defining relationships in Christ.

Personal Question #2: Did God Make My Day?

Focus: Engagement with God in prayer and Scripture.

Core Principle: A personal connection with the heart of God through prayer and the Scriptures gives me both passion and direction for life.

Biblical references: *Proverbs 3:5-6*
                            Mark 1:35
                            John 15:7-8
                            1 John 1:5-7

Please answer this spiritual self-inventory

1=Never 2=Seldom 3=Occasionally 4=Frequently 5=Always

Life-Defining Spiritual Disciplines	Response
1. I regularly read and study my Bible.	1 2 3 4 5
2. When the Bible exposes change needed in my life, I respond to make things right.	1 2 3 4 5
3. I use the Bible as the guide for the way I think and act.	1 2 3 4 5
4. I seriously consider how to obey the voice of God.	1 2 3 4 5
5. I can usually point to a Bible reference that guides me in my choices.	1 2 3 4 5
6. I maintain an attitude of prayer throughout each day.	1 2 3 4 5
7. I have confidence in understanding and interpreting the Bible.	1 2 3 4 5
8. I am usually in a listening posture with God.	1 2 3 4 5
9. I expect God to use me every day in His kingdom work.	1 2 3 4 5
10. I engage in a daily prayer time.	1 2 3 4 5
Did God Make My Day? **TOTAL**	

Made in the USA
Columbia, SC
28 December 2018